Lift Up Your Hearts

A Parish Priest Speaks with his People

– Further Selected Sermons –

Cormac Rigby

FAMILY PUBLICATIONS

OXFORD

ISBN 1-871217-47-4 (hardback)
ISBN 1-871217-48-2 (paperback)

by the same author
The Lord be with You
(also available on CD and audiocassette)

*The author and the publishers wish to express their thanks
to those friends and parishioners who kindly allowed
the use of their illustrations in this book.*

*We are also grateful to the Society of Jesus, Richards Press Ltd.,
and Gerald Duckworth & Co. Ltd. for allowing publication
of extracts from poems by Gerard Manley Hopkins,
A E Housman, Raymond Heywood and Robert Graves.*

Cover photograph by Stephen Patterson.

published by
Family Publications
6a King Street, Oxford, OX2 6DF

printed in England by
Cromwell Press, Trowbridge, Wilts.

Contents

Morningstar

When in the softened chills of breathless dawn
Dark silhouettes swelled into coloured life,
The searcher into feelings newly-born
Feared a new day of test and inward strife.
Low in the frosted sky the morningstar
Glimmered, unhustled by the growing light;
Gently between the dark and day, afar
But ever nearer, soft but oh! so bright.
Dear morningstar, I trusted your warm glow,
And thought to let you guide me through the day,
But ere the sun is risen you must go
And I unlighted go my westering way.
    But see, translated, there you gently are,
    My guide, but beckoning now, bright evening star.

Foreword

I am grateful for the privilege of writing a foreword to this second volume of selected sermons by Fr Cormac.

Having heard him preach on a number of occasions, I have been moved by his wisdom and insight. He has an extraordinary gift of being able to explore the 'Mystery of Faith' and make it accessible to others through his preaching. Drawing on theology, prayer, literature, music and the theatre, he brings fresh insight into our faith.

Fr Cormac makes clear that the sermon is primarily conceived for the spoken word. How many people have delighted to hear him speak that word! He is the first to acknowledge that the sermon is much more than the words of the preacher, no matter how beautifully crafted. In Sermon 22, he describes the dynamic relationship of the one who speaks with the one who listens. He is joined to the congregation which receives a comfort and a challenge in the encounter with the Word of God who is Jesus through the power of His Spirit. Reading these sermons allows time for that word to speak in the silence of our heart.

The poet William Blake captures poetry, prayer and preaching in these wonderful words of his own:

Unless the eye catch fire
The God will not be seen.
Unless the ear catch fire
The God will not be heard
Unless the tongue catch fire
The God will not be loved.
Unless the mind catch fire
The God will not be known.

The words of the sermons contained in *Lift Up Your Hearts* will fill the hearts of all who listen and read them with the fire of God's love.

+ George Stack
Auxiliary Bishop of Westminster

1

About the author

Fr Cormac Rigby is a priest of the Westminster diocese. He has also been an historian of Victorian education, a radio announcer, and a respected writer and broadcaster on ballet.

He was educated at St Theresa's in Rickmansworth, Holy Rood in Watford, and Merchant Taylors'. He was a Sir Thomas White scholar of St John's College, Oxford, where he read Modern History. His doctoral thesis was on the life and influence of the great nineteenth-century teacher, Edward Thring, headmaster of Uppingham 1853–1887.

For twenty years (1965–1985), he was a BBC announcer, the last fourteen of them as Presentation Editor, Radio 3. His deep love of the ballet led to the Radio 3 series *Royal Repertoire*, which ran throughout the 1970s, and to his writing on the ballet for *Dance and Dancers, Set to Music, The Oxford Mail, The Times* and *Dance Now*. He scripted the final programme for *Ballet for All* ('Ashton: The Dream Era') and in 2003 David Bintley dedicated his new ballet *Beauty and the Beast* 'For Cormac'.

Cardinal Basil Hume ordained him on 21 May 1988 and appointed him to be assistant priest at Most Sacred Heart, Ruislip. In 1999 he became Parish Priest of St William of York, Stanmore. He was diagnosed with cancer in 2003 and returned to live in North Oxford.

A collection of his sermons, *The Lord be with You*, was published at the end of 2003 and was so well received that this second selection has now been made.

Preface

I was more than a little surprised that the sermons published as *The Lord be with you* have been so warmly welcomed and I have been greatly heartened by so many different responses to them. My enforced retirement has been put to good use and I thank Denis and Valerie Riches for their determination to bring the sermons to a much wider audience.

This second selection, like the first, is not constrained by any calendar order, but reflects the many different circumstances of the parish sermon. So it includes a wedding and a funeral sermon as well as Sunday sermons prompted by external events – 9/11, for example, and the death of Cardinal Hume.

The parish priest is constantly aware of the need to proclaim the Gospel in the context of people's lives. Good communicators know they have to listen carefully before they can speak effectively. The first duty of the preacher is to offer the timeless truths and values of the Faith and to do so effectively by giving the hearers evidence that their circumstances and experiences are perceived and understood.

I have been sustained since I retired by many friends, particularly among my former parishioners in Ruislip and Stanmore.

I owe more than I can ever express in words to Kevin O'Hare, Willie Skehan, David McLellan, Brian Harrison, David Bintley, Roger Warren and Mark Wynter.

Cormac Rigby
Oxford, July 2004

On the 16th anniversary of his ordination, 21 May 2004,
Fr Cormac was able to celebrate Mass at the Oratory of St Finbarr
on the island at Gougane Barra, County Cork.
Photograph by Lee Doherty.

Chapter 1

Unless a wheat grain falls to the ground and dies
it remains only a single grain; but if it dies, it yields a rich harvest.

For so many of our fellow-countrymen
death is the end of everything, the final curtain.
For followers of Christ there is a profoundly different perception.

The body that goes into the grave is like the grain of wheat
going into the soil. Its life is not over.
Only now can its purpose be fulfilled.
For Christians death is inevitable, but not final;
a fact of life, but not the end of life.

Jesus showed us how it happens. He died on the cross.
Of that we can be in no doubt. They had no need to break
his legs; but to make absolutely certain, they pierced his side
and drained his body of every last drop of blood.
His body could not have been more dead.

But on Easter morning Jesus was alive.
Not a phantom, not a ghost – a man of flesh and blood.
And that is what changes everything.

In this everyday world of ours, we tend to look ahead,
to see where we're going – but, alas, when we look towards
the future we see all too clearly the horizon of death.
It may be very close; it may be miles away.
But when we look west we see the place where our sun will set
and it looks like a final moment.

For so many people the end of life is the sometimes magnificent,
but always melancholy glory of the sunset. Christians, however,
look in the opposite direction – towards the sunrise.

Sunrise here on earth begins in the east and eternity's sunrise
comes from the east too. So our orientation as Christians is

literally what sets us apart. For us Christians the purpose of life
is the dawning realisation of our permanent value to God
in his eternal sunrise. Looked at from where he is
our earthly sunset is his eternal sunrise.

We are the Easter people, the people of the sunrise, and when the
great saint Augustine finished his sermons he would often urge
his listeners to turn to the East, to pray, turning to face the Lord.

It became common practice to build Christian churches –
in the days when land was no problem – to build them
so that the people would look towards the sunrise.
And there's a moment in the Mass when I say cheerfully to you
"Lift up your hearts", "Sursum corda", and you respond –
equally cheerfully – "We lift them up to the Lord" –
and in the early days of the church you'd likely turn
towards the east as you said that: turning to the Lord;
facing east, facing the Lord.

According to Tertullian, round about the year 200 it was
common Christian practice to face the east in prayer.
He speaks of Christians "praying in the direction of the
rising sun", and people would actually indicate the direction
by making a cross on the wall of their house.

Such a cross was found in an upstairs room of a house
in the city of Herculaneum buried by the eruption of
Mount Vesuvius in 79AD – when the beloved disciple
St John was still alive and preaching about Jesus.

St John Chrysostom described how the faithful of his time,
during the Canon of the Mass, would turn to gaze out through
the open doors, doors through which the light of the rising sun
streamed in. In Ireland there grew up a tradition of burying
Christian folk with their head towards the west, so that
when they rise from the dead they may face the rising sun.

The phrase became the title of a great novel by
John McGahern, *That They May Face the Rising Sun*.

But do you know, I suspect that nowadays many of our
town-dwelling children have only the haziest idea of where
east and west are. Wouldn't it be a good idea this Eastertide
to think about it with them – to be aware of east and west,
sunrise and sunset?

Anyone who has to navigate at sea or in the air – or even on the
road – needs to be aware of the compass points. As we navigate
our way through life we don't need to be crying "Westward Ho"
and consoling ourselves with a sunset. We need to look east,
to the Lord rising from the tomb to launch eternal life.

It would be good this Passiontide to discover where in our
own homes the east is and to mark it as our ancestors did, with a
cross or a crucifix. The sunrise in the east is the expression of
our hope and the fulfilment of our destiny.
Christ is our morning-star

> "Praise with elation, praise ev'ry morning
>   God's re-creation of the new day."

That is what we'll be celebrating at Easter:
God's re-creation of our new day.

Our days on earth are numbered and are running out.
The eternal sunrise is what we're waiting for,
and even in the still of the night we have the sense of anticipation:

> "I watch the moonlight guarding the night,
>   waiting till morning comes".

Easter ends the power of darkness
and the Risen Lord comes to us from the east.

> "Let him easter in us, be a dayspring to the dimness of us,
>   be a crimson-cresseted east."

The grain must die to yield its rich harvest.

*"Uncle Frank, Francis McCormack, that fine eldest
brother whom his young sister, my mother, adored;
so full of talents that were never used."*

Chapter 2

You entrusted me with five talents;
here are five more that I have made.

In a way, it's all too easy to preach about using talents.

No argument really. God gave each of us
our own range of gifts, and it's up to us
to make full use of our opportunities.
End of sermon.

But all this week I've been thinking about my uncle Frank.
He was my mother's eldest brother and he was many-talented.
He was bright and intelligent and good-humoured, and he was
a good athlete too – a long-distance runner.

But when he died, just fifty years ago, he was a shambling
wreck. I was only ten when he died and I feel terribly ashamed
as I look back now, at how little I did for him.

To he honest, I was frightened to go near him. He sat at the
corner of the table in Granny and Grandad's house in St Helens,
his head slumped on his chest, his eyes unfocussed, and unable
to speak – he just mumbled. They had to help him to eat.
I hated having to be near him – and that's what makes me
feel so ashamed now.

When the First World War started in 1914 the bright and bold
young Francis, still a teenager, was one of the first to volunteer
to join the army and defend his country. He was a great runner
and could be very useful.

But fate was not kind to him.

That 'War to end all Wars' ended in 1918, but his life didn't end
till 1949. For thirty-one years he was a living reminder of the
horror of war. He wasn't wounded; he hadn't lost a limb.

But in the trenches he was badly gassed and it destroyed the rest
of his life. That fine eldest brother whom his sister, my mother,
adored, went away to war an athlete and came back a ruin.
If only I had been able to understand that properly I might
have made more effort to understand his mutterings and
to forget his dribbling and to try to show him some affection
and understanding. But I was only nine and I didn't understand.

You won't find his name on a War Memorial
because by the time he eventually found peace in the grave,
there'd been a long peace and a second World War.
He hadn't been killed outright, so he wasn't a name
on a monument. He was just human debris. The gas that
choked him in the trenches burned the inside of his lungs
and finally killed him thirty years later. For three decades his
parents and his brothers and sister coped with that living death.

On Remembrance Day, I like to remember his youthful courage.
I like to remember the young fellow in the photos, so full of
talents that were never used. And I have to remember the way
I didn't help, when I was a boy. And he says to me across
the fifty years since he died:

> It's not enough to preach on this parable of the talents
> and to say it's up to everyone to use their own gifts
> to the fullest. That's only part of what Jesus meant.
> God gave me five talents and the only one I was able
> to use was my courage: I was robbed of the chance
> to use all my other gifts.

> In your sermon you have to say that we must be
> responsible for other people's talents as well as our own.
> And you must do everything in your power to ensure
> that never again are the talents of such a young fellow
> to be blighted and wasted in the way mine were.

He's right. If I only concern myself with my own talents,
I'm no better than the man who buried his talents in the ground.
I have to spend my talents, spend my energy, spend my life
to create a better world in which all talents are developed
and no human life is wasted.

I remember Uncle Frank in the minute's silence and I vow
to do everything in my power to make sure that no young lad
today suffers as he suffered.

If we fail to live our lives positively working for peace,
we are the ones who deserve to be thrown into the dark
where there is weeping and grinding of teeth.

I ask my uncle, dead these fifty years, to inspire me,
and to inspire you, to work for peace.

*The robin and the wing-mirror. After hearing this sermon, Anne Rourke,
a parishioner at Ruislip, painted this watercolour and gave it to Father Cormac.*

Chapter 3

Anyone who loves his life loses it.

You think of the robin as a bright-eyed, red-breasted, cheerful little songster who gets his picture on the front of countless Christmas cards.

That may be his image at Christmas – but in the spring a young robin's fancy lightly turns to thoughts of love – well, mating. And actually it isn't very loving; more a matter of possessing, owning, asserting his ownership over a patch, a territory. And not 'lightly' either but murderously, aggressively.

If you wander past the front door of the Presbytery, you'll see my little green Golf parked outside. Take a look at both wing-mirrors and you'll think I must have parked it under a tree because the door is liberally spattered with bird-droppings.

And then take a closer look and you'll see that the mirrors themselves are smeared. Quite a mess really.

I looked out one morning last week and saw the explanation. A robin was perched on the mirror angrily attacking the robin inside the mirror. The robin was beside itself with rage that this intruder was on its patch. It flew at the mirror, stabbing at the mirror with its beak – and the more it attacked, the more the bird in the mirror attacked back!

And when it got exhausted on one side of the car it flew over to the other and attacked the robin in that mirror too. The mirrors are beak-bashed and the droppings testify to the continuing nature of the onslaught. All that energy, all that hostility spent on protecting its patch from a mirror-image.

And that's what we're like too.

Our aggression, our defensiveness, our determination to be in
the right, our obsession with ourselves and our possessions
put us in the same category as the robin attacking my car.
So angrily possessive, so belligerent at imagined threats,
that we don't realise it's ourselves we're attacking.
We get so worked up defending something of ours against
all comers that we don't see it's only ourselves we're hitting.

What is original sin?
What did Adam and Eve do in the Garden?
Forget about scrumping apples:
that's just a way of putting it.

Adam's sin was to put himself in the centre of his world.
And he was so obsessed by his own selfish wish to do anything
he felt like doing, that he defied God and ate the forbidden fruit.

He put himself first, God second, and everyone else also-ran.
He deluded himself – as the robin deluded itself – that he had
to protect Number One. And it is a delusion,
the oldest delusion in the world.

The man who thinks it's himself against God, himself against
the rest of the world, is a fallen man, fallen from grace, failing
to understand how God's creation works. He deludes himself,
imagines he's got to attack all opponents and fails to realise
that the arch-opponent in the wing-mirror is in fact himself.

He thinks he loves his life so much that he's saving it.
Saving it! From God! And from his fellow-men! In fact
he's wasting his energy attacking his own self in the mirror.

Whenever you hear of marriage break-downs, family feuds,
sibling run-ins, the chances are that at the centre of it
is someone thinking he or she is standing up for himself or herself.
Putting myself first, putting my needs at the centre,
attacking those who get in my way.

And the tragedy is that the only one who really gets in my way
is me – my blinkered vision, my deluded notion,
my failure to perceive that the real threat against my well-being
comes not from any other member of the family,
or God, but from the person I see in the mirror.

The sin of Adam puts self first, God is ignored, neighbours
pushed back. Self rules – and when self rules, happiness goes
out of the window. The message of the second Adam, Jesus,
is forget self. If you lose your selfish life, you gain love,
and if you gain love, you win a new world of happiness.

The person who deliberately turns his or her back on the values
of the world and puts love of God first, the person who
decisively rejects self and puts love of others top of the agenda,
is the one who discovers true fulfilment and true happiness.

So, if you wander past my car today and see the signs of that
pathetic battle of self against self, remember what a perfect
image it is of our own deluded priorities. Blindly, stupidly
defending self against all comers, we destroy only ourselves.
Seeing the world clearly as our reason for forgetting self
and loving others, loving God, loving family, loving neighbours,
we fulfill ourselves and bring our lives through all the struggles
to the glory of Easter morning.

"Good news to preach and good tunes to broadcast."
Cormac Rigby, Presentation Editor, Radio 3, in the radio box
at the Royal Albert Hall, introducing a live broadcast of one of the Proms.

Chapter 4

John came to you, a pattern of true righteousness
but you did not believe him

I really ought to be at the Festival Hall tonight for the
concert marking the fiftieth birthday of Radio 3.

The concert includes Janacek's gripping Glagolitic Mass –
but (as you see) I'm saying Mass here instead
so I can genuinely say to my old colleagues
I'm with you in spirit.

When I left the BBC in 1985, I remember joking
that the difference between the Catholic Church
and the BBC was that in the Catholic Church
it's only the one man at the very top who is infallible.

But, in fact, nailing my colours to the Catholic Church
has a lot in common with the nailing of my colours to
Radio 3 and the Third Programme.

For a start, you have to recognise that you're in a minority.
Very few people tune in to Radio 3; very few of our fellow
countrymen come to Mass. On the other hand, those who
do belong are very strongly motivated. Hell has no fury
like a Third Programme listener hearing a split infinitive;
hell has no fury like a Catholic who gets the presbytery
answering machine.

But seriously – in both my lives I've been working for an ideal.
The Third Programme believed it improved the quality of life.
So does the Catholic Church.

The Third Programme said: we believe this is worth hearing;
we're not going to cut it to fit a slot; we're not going to jazz
it up, and we're not going to hype you into listening to it.

It's yours if you choose to tune in; but the choice is yours.
We don't judge our programmes by the size of audience
they attract. If it's good, and people know it's there,
they'll come to it when they're ready.
Popularity as such doesn't really matter.

And I think the same is true of the Faith.
If Radio 3 wanted a bigger audience for its early morning
concert, they could hire Terry Wogan to present it.
The audience would increase but they'd be there for Wogan,
not for the music. The music has its natural constituency
and gimmicks won't alter that.

If Radio 3 keeps its nerve and keeps its reputation for
broadcasting the best, without blarney or sales patter,
the people who want to try a bit of Mozart, or Haydn, or
Britten will know where it is and tune in when they want it.

Our job wasn't to pretend that classical music is trendy,
or chic, or relevant but just worth listening to, and therefore
worth broadcasting. A serious purpose – though we didn't
take ourselves too seriously.

One of my great pals was Ray Moore who'd be chatting up
the millions on Radio 2 while I was serving Satie to the few
on Radio 3.

He loved to send us up. He'd imagine the Radio 3 studio
like the Palm Court of Grand Hotel with aspidistras over
the gramophones and doilies under the coffee cups.
And he'd be amazed that most of the music we were serving up
was by composers who were dead! Or had rude names
like Shütz and Scheidt or Smetana or Poulenc.

If you go in to Radio 3 in the morning, he'd say, there'd be an
awful whiff of Poo-lonk. Somebody had already trodden some
'orrible dollops of Poo-lonk into the rush matting and you could

smell it in Portland Place, and Patricia Hughes would have to put on her best dual-strength Harrods' rubber gloves and seize the offending Poo-lonk with stainless steel tweezers and slide it onto the spare gramophone – and always remember to wash her hands in Fairy Liquid afterwards.

Great fun! There is undoubtedly a certain pomposity about serious-music-lovers which needs to be laughed out of court. But it didn't affect our basic confidence in the value of what we were doing.

And that is true of the Church too. It would be very easy to dress up the Gospel and make it look great fun. Happy-clappy sing-a-long-a-Jesus. We could cut all Masses to 10 minutes of soul music and laser displays. We could forget about boring old dogmas and chuck out outmoded ethics and tell people it's OK to do your own thing. We could say if it's made a profit, God must be with it. We could say adultery's OK, it's just a new concept of self-fulfilment.

It's the easiest thing in the world to be popular – but popularity is not our goal.

Radio 3 is content to say: here is a diet of speech and music, if you select from it sensibly it will expand your horizons, deepen your perceptions, and make life a better experience.

And the Church says much the same: Here is a gospel which is a joy to believe, and a terrific effort to live but a consolation in sorrow and distress. Here is a philosophy of life which is hard to pursue but definitely rewarding. Here are values which lose out in the market place but which will carry you unscathed through the slings and arrows of outrageous fortune. Here is a Gospel of Love Crucified.

We're not going to dress Jesus up as a pop star.
We're content to let the Cross speak its own message.

We don't expect it to become trendy with the night-club ravers and the expense account brigade. But we know it will speak to the heartbroken and the neglected.

The important thing is the integrity of the message.

Yes – John came and preached a pattern of true righteousness and you ignored him – but that doesn't invalidate John's message.

Those who broadcast know the worth of their material, be it classical music or the Gospel of Jesus. And they know that most will ignore it and will not tune in. But they persevere.

It's easy to pander to popular taste but it's a fatal mistake to get with it. What people long for, deep down, is the security of a lifetime's consolation.

We have good news to preach and good tunes to broadcast. Our song is love unknown.

Happy Birthday, Radio 3. Happy Birthday, Sacred Heart.

Chapter 5

Search and you will find.

The whole of life is a searching process. I'm searching for the answer to the most basic questions. What's the purpose of it all? What should I be doing to make the best of it?

Answers aren't instant. You can't simply flick a switch and *know*. If you want to know a fact – when did Henry VIII reign? – you go to your books, or these days you find a website, and there's the answer: 1509–1547.

If you want to understand a reason, if you want to understand what makes one person love another, it's a much longer process. Getting to know oneself – one's motives, one's feelings, one's strengths and weaknesses – is a lifetime's search.

And part of that search for understanding is searching for love, searching for God. You don't open a door and find God. You don't win an argument and prove God. And God hasn't got his own website.

God isn't just some fact. God is a mystery. God is a mystery, because God is love and we don't know nearly enough about love.

Some people fall in love with a pretty face, but a pretty face isn't the whole person, and personhood is a vast and complex mystery. To love someone is to be intrigued by their mystery and to want to approach it and to understand it more and more. And yet at the same time you have to recognise that you can never totally understand another person, even your nearest and dearest.

So the search for understanding is a long one. And if it is difficult to penetrate the mystery of another person, how much more difficult to penetrate the mystery of God.

The more I love someone, the more curious I am about him; the more questions I ask, the more I want to know, because I realise I can't really love him if I don't understand him.

And so love is a searching – not for facts, although those are important, but for understanding. I love and therefore I long to understand. And so if I'm serious about loving God, I'll long to understand God.

If I want to understand why he created me, if I want to know what he expects of me, if I want to see where our relationship is going, I have to search. I have to do all I can to delve deeper into the meaning of love.

So yes, I'll go to the shelves and websites for the facts, for the history and philosophy and the theology – but I also need to go to those with understanding. I'll need to listen to poetry and music, to Shakespeare and Mozart: other people's insights – the experience of others more spiritually alert than I can ever be: the poets, the saints and the composers.

I need to listen to them all. *Listen* to them. But the most important person to listen to is God himself.

Prayer. Too many people think that prayer is bombarding God with requests. We tend to pray by verbal assault. There is indeed a time for asking our father for our needs and there is a time for praising him. But most of all, there's a time for shutting up and listening to him.

We should beware of filling our prayers with pious clatter, and choose silence and peace so that we can listen deliberately to what he's saying. Come early for Mass – and greet your friends in the colonnade and the porch; but when you come into the church, preserve the peace.

Be still, listen. Don't create noise: create silence and stillness, create awareness of God's presence.

Let your eyes focus on the crucifix or the tabernacle;
allow the Lord eye-to-eye contact and let him whisper in your ear.

At Mass we stand and kneel to pray together – and quite right too.
But we also need to sit or kneel by ourselves: just me and God,
and silence, and let him do the talking.

What posture should we adopt? Maybe it's good to kneel and
look up – to raise our eyes, as well as our minds and hearts,
to God. Or maybe it's good to sit quietly and close our eyes,
so that God doesn't have to compete with other distractions.
We each have to find our own way of doing it: what's best for us.

What we have to remember is that true prayer is a dialogue –
it takes two to pray.

Sometimes I imagine Jesus sitting across the table from me,
conversing with me in the way I'm used to talking with my
friends over a meal. That sort of prayer is conversation.

Sometimes I imagine Jesus walking beside me – can't see him,
except out of the corner of my eye. But as we walk together,
through the woods, in the gardens, by the lakeshore, the thoughts
come and go: some of them are my thoughts, some are his.

Sometimes he's my passenger and we talk as I drive, especially
on long journeys on roads I know.

Sometimes he's my guest at concerts, and when he hears
something of penetrating beauty he draws my attention to it.

Sometimes he nudges me when I'm reading and my thoughts
spiral on from something I've read, into a sudden insight of my own.
I'm always ready to keep the conversation going, but I have
to remember to shut up and let him get a word in edgeways.

Searching is a silent process, really.
You don't understand better
by constantly saying you don't understand.

You understand better when you make the effort to listen.
Listening is the key to mystery. Listening is the secret of
understanding. Listening is the doorway to happiness.

Almost exactly four hundred years ago, Sir John Falstaff
put his finger on his own problem: he was forever blustering
his way through life and making a fuss and a rumpus.

> "It's the disease of not listening," he admitted –
> "the disease of not listening, the malady of not marking
> that I am troubled withal."

We all suffer from that disease of not listening.

As Oliver Wendell Holmes wrote:

> It is the province of knowledge to speak,
> and it is the privilege of wisdom to listen.

Chapter 6

See that you are dressed for action and have your lamps lit.

Some people feel threatened by the basic Christian philosophy,
our awareness that death may take us at any time
and we must therefore be ready. It's morbid, they think.
They feel that awareness of death is a denial of life.

Precisely the opposite is true.
Loving life in a state of being prepared
actually gives us a tremendous freedom.

Obituaries list the achievement and possessions of life,
but the real test of a life is to ask about the spirit
in which that life is lived.

I'm at the age now when retirement is both desirable –
and appropriate! I can look back at the group of people
with whom I shared my student days and I remember
our high hopes. I look at the same people now as they
gradually retire from their jobs and professions and I see
all sorts of mixtures of failure and success. But again
and again what really seems important is not what will
appear in the obituaries but my perception of the spirit
in which they have lived their lives.

I've one friend in particular who is a prodigiously gifted
academic with many books to his credit – a definitive
biography, many textbooks – a man in demand as lecturer
in America and China. But what his friends most admire
in him is the generosity with which he gives his time.

Many people behave like misers with their time –
so busy hoarding it that they never spend it.
Time is the real measure of our lives.

Today is my only spendable currency.
Yesterday is in the bank and I can't do anything with it.
Tomorrow is futures that could be vastly over-valued.
It's only today I can spend freely.
And that's why Christians live for today.

This moment is my gift from God –
and if I can give this moment to others for love of them,
then I'm using time to best effect.

Being prepared and being dressed for action and having
one's lamps lit, isn't because we're scared of being caught out,
isn't because death is lurking to scare us. It's recognising
that time is God's gift – and there's no time like the present.
The worst thing someone can say is "I've no time for him ..."

When I think of my mother's long life, what I remember most
is the time she gave to me. Children don't really remember
whether their parents were rich or poor.
They remember whether or not they had time for them.

Giving time is far more generous than giving money.
Living each moment is taking care of the pence of our lives.
Don't let's worry about the pounds – the career structures,
the marriages, the life strategy. Let's concentrate on the pence,
the here and now.

> Lord, for tomorrow and its needs I do not pray.
> Keep me my God from stain of sin, just for today.

Time is my gift from God – a time I have at my disposal.
I can hug it to myself – or I can share it. I can be a miser –
or a benefactor. Time is what I need to use most wisely.
I don't want to use it like a spendthrift,
but nor must I be a Scrooge.
I want to give it its best value.
I want to invest it in happiness and fulfilment.

I had no idea when I came to Ruislip that I'd be here for a whole decade. I look back on those ten years with great gladness. But already, it's history, it's in the Bank. And today – and everyday – I've only got today to spend.

It's not the length of life that matters nor the cost of living but the spirit in which I live my life. And to live life happily is to spend time with the generosity of friendship. Where your treasure is, there will your heart be also. That's the key to it.

Being ready for death isn't morbid. It's living life to the full, loving every moment of it and giving as much time as possible to the love of friends. If every moment is truly being lived to its fullest potential, it doesn't matter when death comes. It's not daunting to think of death. It's not gloomy to live each day as if it were the last.

> Let me in season, Lord, be grave; in season gay.
> Let me be faithful to thy Grace, just for today.

*Every wedding is different. Some couples like gatherings of the clans
and a full church; others prefer the intimacy of a sanctuary wedding,
with only immediate family and closest friends. That is for each couple to decide.
And the priest happily adapts, rejoicing that the life of the newly-weds will be consciously
launched in the house of God. It was a particular joy for Fr Cormac, in his retirement,
to be invited to celebrate Nuptial Mass for Liz Browning and Cormac Purtill.*

Chapter 7

Remain in my love.

Sermon preached at St John Fisher, Rochester, at the Nuptial Mass for Cormac Purtill and Liz Browning, 7 February 2004.

You probably know
that I first met Cormac
quite a long time ago,
because of our shared Christian name.
And when Cormac the boy
was confirmed by Cormac the bishop,
he invited me to be Cormac the sponsor.

I was given the name Cormac because my mother's maiden name
was McCormack – and that explains why so many of the records
we played on our old wind-up gramophone when I was a boy
were the recordings made by Count John McCormack.

I loved them then and I love them still. And my favourite is the
gentle ballad by Charles Marshall which John McCormack was
the first to sing. Its title is a mantra which has lingered with me
all my life; the images of love which it conjures up move me still:

> I'll walk beside you, through the world today,
> While dreams and songs and flowers bless your way;
> I'll look into your eyes and hold your hand.
> I'll walk beside you through the golden land.

It seems right to evoke that image today as Cormac and Liz
set out on their journey together through the rest of life.
And it seems particularly apt because that is how they first
saw one another: walking together from St Anne's to the Chaplaincy
for Mass on Cormac's first Sunday in Oxford, young people
anchoring their lives in the practice of the faith. They have
remained in that love of God and, please God, they always will.

Our secular friends describe a wedding as the moment when two people 'tie the knot' or 'sign the contract' and that's true enough. But we Christians believe that a wedding is the moment when two people recognise that their love needs to be strengthened and eternalised by God – and St John tells us that God is Love.

If that is the case, then it makes sense to grace our human love with the creative power of that divine love.

In the words of the Preface of this Mass: Love is man's origin; love is his constant calling; love is his fulfilment in heaven. The love of man and woman is made holy by the sacrament of marriage, and becomes the mirror of God's everlasting love.

That's quite a perception.

What could give more courage to a bride and groom than to see their love as God sees it: as a mirror reflecting his love into the world and sharing his creative Life of Love.

Through the sacrament of marriage, the grace of God touches and strengthens the shared life of the couple. This isn't wedding day pie-in-the-sky. We know that the future will bring good things and bad – and it is precisely because of that mature realism that the Church sees the absolute necessity of bringing the grace of God, his inner strength, into the equation.

The purpose of a wedding
is to make that grace visible today
and memorable throughout their lives.

Cormac and Liz have chosen to walk alongside one another – but they do not walk alone. That unending circle of gold which they will place on one another's fingers symbolises the unending love of God which will sustain and strengthen their love. Not just for this hour, not for just a day, not for just a year, but always.

It sounds powerful when they make their vows: to love and
to cherish, till death do us part. The promise they make to
one another is supported by the promise God makes to them.
Remain in my love, He says, so that your joy may be complete.

Liz and Cormac – you are both blessed in having before you
indicators of the truth of what I have been saying:
the marriages of your own parents.

Good marriages, we're often told, are *made* in heaven.
And so they are – but they evolve day to day here on earth.
They evolve when the couple love and trust one another
and love and trust God.

I can hear God's voice in the last verse of that ballad:

> I'll walk beside you through the passing years
> Through days of cloud and sunshine, joys and tears.
> And when the great call comes, though sunset gleams,
> I'll walk beside you to the land of dreams.

Remain in His Love.

Chapter 8

Let the little children come to me.

Ciara died early in August quite some time before she was due
to be born, but her twin brother was still growing in the womb.
And so we were grieving for her at the same time as we were
hoping for him.

We have no problem with the death of an innocent – in the sense
that we are confident that the fulfilment which eluded her on earth
is already hers now with God.

We feel no apprehension, no anxiety, no concern for her
because "God has taken her into his loving care".
Though we can't help feeling pangs of regret that we had no time
with her, we know that the joy of meeting her and getting to know
her is a joy postponed until we all reach eternity.

It was on the evening of August 25th that her brother was born
into the world and, in a way, his name chose itself. Among the
Apostles of Jesus was Thomas, the Twin, the devoted brother.

Thomas was born safely and is flourishing now, thank God.
I was moved myself by his birth because at the very hour when
Thomas was coming into the world my mother was departing
from it. There was such a beautiful configuration of providence
which linked the start of the little one's life on earth with the
start of the old lady's life in Heaven.

Life doesn't end at death:
for those who die in Christ it changes for the better.
Life with God, for Ciara and for my mother.
Life on earth for Thomas.
The closeness of events made its own point,
and it's the central point of our faith:
each life extinguished on earth
should be a new star kindled in heaven.

And the shortness or length of life is of no great consequence
because the lady of ninety-four years
and the lady who lived only in the womb
are equally beloved of God.

It's lovely too that this Requiem for an innocent takes place
on the Friday of the parish mission. The church will be packed
with children tonight, coming along to bring a flower for Mary
our Mother. The innocent love of childhood is the country
of which Mary is Queen, and if we are to reach that country
ourselves – that kingdom of God, that province of Mary –
we have to recapture the innocence of childhood ourselves.

Shortly we'll be singing the hymn to Our Lady which catches
that blithe innocence, and it's good to make it a celebration
of Ciara, the flower Mary has gathered to herself.

Ciara's place in her parents' hearts will always be secure.
Her place in her twin brother's life will be as a guiding star.
When Thomas grows older he'll be as close to Ciara
as St Francis was to St Clare, close in spirit.

Ciara Josephine – her second name was her grandmother's;
the plan is to take the ashes over to Larne and to bury them
in her grandmother's grave for safekeeping till the resurrection.

For all of us at Mass this morning there are two prayers we must
say: the first is to pray for the safety and well-being of Thomas who
will be baptised on Sunday; and the second is to thank God for the
influence of Ciara whom God has taken into his loving care.

The disciples didn't want Jesus to be pestered by children.
But Jesus had other and better ideas: let the children come to me.

I think of Ciara and her grandmother in heaven now.
I think of my mother there too and all of them praying
with us this morning, praying with us and for us,
and especially for Thomas the Twin.

Pope Pius XII

Eugenio Pacelli was born on 2 March 1876 and elected Pope on 2 March 1939.
Fr Cormac took this photo on 4 September 1957 at Castelgandolfo.

"A great barrage of cheering and waving greeted him; I felt charged with love for him
but I could not cheer. I found myself mouthing voicelessly 'God bless you, God bless you'
and tears streamed down my cheeks. He sat down and talked to us — first in Italian,
then French, English, German, Spanish. Each nation waved and cheered as he ended.
Then he stood and slowly gave us his blessing."

Pope Pius XII died at Castelgandolfo on 5 October 1958.

Chapter 9

Refute falsehood, correct error.

I've been celebrating this month the fortieth anniversary
of the most significant milestone in my life. It's forty years
since I went up to university and took charge of my own life.

The day I went up to Oxford the papers were full of the news
that the Pope was dying. I'd seen Pope Pius XII at
Castelgandolfo the previous summer and will never forget
the impact it made.

I decided on my first evening in Oxford that I'd get up early
the next morning and go to Mass and pray for him. I discovered
a Catholic church only a few minutes walk from College and
it had an early Mass at 7.15. When I emerged from Mass and
went into the newsagent the papers all had the same headline:
The Pope is Dead.

My first night in Oxford was the Pope's first night in heaven,
and so from that moment on I thought of him as my special patron,
and I've been a daily mass-goer ever since.

I was born in May 1939 and Pius XII had been elected Pope
in March, so in 1958 he was the only Pope I'd ever known –
rather as Pope John Paul II is to young people today.

Pope Pius XII was a Roman, born into an aristocratic family,
the Pacellis. He was a frail-looking young man with deep
brown eyes – a slightly ethereal look. At one time it
looked as if his delicate health might prevent him training
for the priesthood. But eventually he was ordained, in 1899,
and became a member of the papal diplomatic service.

His most difficult and dangerous posting was as papal nuncio
in Bavaria, where at one point in 1918 Communist insurgents

broke into the nunciature in Munich and threatened to kill him. Pacelli faced them calmly and survived. He did not lack courage.

His first-hand knowledge of Germany throughout the 1920s made him very valuable to Pope Pius XI who was coping with the problem of how the Church should react to the rise of fascism in Germany – and in Italy too.

Pacelli became a Cardinal and Pius XI's Secretary of State in 1930. Diplomatic efforts to contain the evil of Hitler were mainly unsuccessful and the Pope and the Cardinal decided on a major attack on Nazism. This was the encyclical published in March 1937 denouncing Nazi beliefs as fundamentally unchristian, and its politics as unacceptable. For example, the Nazis banned the Old Testament from schools, as part of their hatred for the Jews. The Pope denounced that.

Remember, this was 1937 when most English politicians were more likely to be appeasing Hitler than standing up to him.

So determined was the Vatican to make its position unequivocal that the letter wasn't published in Latin but in the language of the people who needed to hear it: the Germans.
Mit brennender Sorge: with burning anxiety. Copies were smuggled into Germany and many priests risked physical violence from Nazi party members to read it from their pulpits on Palm Sunday. From that moment it was clear that there was enmity between Nazi Germany and the Catholic Church.

At the Nuremberg trials after the war, Hitler's foreign minister Ribbentrop complained that there had been a whole desk full of protests from the Vatican against Nazi activities.

In the spring of 1939 Pius XI died and on 2nd March, his 63rd birthday, Eugenio Pacelli was elected to succeed him. He took the name Pius XII to signify continuity with the views and policies of his predecessor.

In September 1939 World War II began and Pius XII became effectively surrounded by Mussolini's Italy, which soon began to imitate Hitler's anti-Jewish policy.

There was a round-up of Jews in Rome itself. The Pope angrily summoned the German ambassador's assistant, von Kessel. He was one of the many decent Germans appalled by what was being done. He begged the Pope to soft-pedal – defiance would only make matters worse for the Jews.

His ambassador sent a message back to Berlin saying the Pope would not make a public protest. And the ploy worked. It gave seven thousand Jews in Rome time to hide, many of them in convents and monasteries which the Fascists were reluctant to enter by force. The Pope suspended the normal rules of the cloister so that shelter could be given.

Was the Pope wise not to make a public protest? He had heard what had happened in Holland. When the first round-up of Jews happened there, the Dutch Catholic bishops made a fierce public protest. The Nazi authorities were so infuriated that they retaliated with increased brutality. They rounded up even Jews who had become Catholics, among them Edith Stein, the Carmelite, canonised last month as a martyr. That protest by the bishops had simply resulted in a "We'll show them" response: more arrests, more deaths.

And it was the same in Poland. The Archbishop of Cracow received a strong note of protest from the Pope, but said that he dared not publish it because it would only make a bad situation worse.

In Holland, 79% of Dutch Jews died. But in neighbouring Belgium, where the Church didn't make noisy protests but got on with undercover rescue, 73% of Belgian Jews survived.

When the war finally ended, many people regarded Pius XII
as the saviour of the city of Rome. But had he achieved that by
betraying the Jews? Among my books I have the autobiography
of the wartime Chief Rabbi of Rome, who was so grateful for
the Pope's efforts to save his people's lives that he actually became
a Christian himself and took the Pope's baptismal name, Eugenio.

It's all too easy to make denunciatory speeches –
the essential thing is to save lives.

In 1964, twenty years after the War, a German playwright wrote
a play attacking Pius XII for not making a stronger moral gesture
against the Holocaust. Ironic – an attack from a German, not
on the appeasers, not on collaborators, but on the author of
Mit Brennender Sorge. Ironic – but it has largely worked.

Again and again you hear good people regretting the so-called
"silence" of Pius XII. Earlier this year a play at Stratford clearly
took it for granted that the slander was true. The playwright,
whom I greatly admire, had simply not realised that, while
Neville Chamberlain was chatting to Hitler, *Mit Brennender Sorge*
was attacking Hitler. Maybe he didn't know of the thousands
of Jews who survived because the Church did so much to
shelter them from persecutions once war had started.

Those who still criticise Pius XII for inactivity should read
Martin Gilbert's book on Auschwitz. The biographer of Churchill
notes how in 1941 the allies knew that the holocaust was going on
but feared that, if they let on, the Germans would realise their codes
were being broken. And so the allies didn't even bomb the railway
line to Auschwitz – the line along which so many death trains passed.

There's a time for speaking out, and there's a time for shutting up.

The time for speaking out is when there's a chance of preventing evil.
The time for speaking out against the Nazis was 1937,
when Pius XI and Pacelli did speak out in *Mit Brennender Sorge*.
Hitler was angry – but Britain and France did nothing.

By the time *Mit Brennender Sorge* was proved to have been right in 1941, the world was at war and millions of Jews were in mortal peril. It would have been so easy for Pius XII to have joined the allied war effort in 1941 with some useful propaganda, but by then words were powerless and practical help was what was needed – and what Pius XII gave.

We should be proud of his speaking out in 1937 and of his shutting up in 1941.

"It's the happiest day of all to be at the wedding of your grandchild."
Laura Cunningham (seated) with her family.
Photograph by Michael Douglas Photography

Chapter 10

Lord, if you had been here . . .

Both the sisters, Martha and Mary – chalk and cheese, but
equally loved by Jesus – they both used exactly the same phrase:
"Lord, if you had been here my brother would not have died."

It was almost a reproach. When Mary repeated it, Jesus
broke down and wept because it showed how much
they had trusted him.

But when Martha says it, Jesus is strong.

"Your brother will rise again", he says.
"Yes, I know – on the last day", she replies

His reply to that is awesome:

"I am the resurrection and the life." –

and in that one sentence addressed to Martha he identifies
himself as our way through death.

On this certain hope, on this assertion by Jesus, the whole
of Christianity rests. Like Lazarus, like Martha and Mary,
like Jesus himself, we will die; but beyond our death
lies the "sure and certain hope" of resurrection and life.

Our tears today are for the separation death brings – but Laura
herself faced death with serenity – she had had a good life,
and a long one and the next sequence did not faze her at all.

Laura seemed to me both Mary and Martha. She was the
wise woman, the contemplative who fell in love with the
beauty of the world seen from the mountain tops. And she
was also the Martha, the practical housewife, down to earth,
humane, tolerant, amused, the Mummy and the Grandma.

I knew her for only the last three of her eighty-five years,
when the always-active woman was confined to her chair;
but it wasn't at all difficult to see where her acceptance
came from. She was amused when people rang her from Italy
– as they often did – and expressed amazement that she wasn't
full of lamentations. But that wasn't her style: she shrugged
and smiled and watched the world go by, and thanked God
for her store of happy memories. She appreciated that
she had no need to worry; she handed over the practicalities
and felt completely secure. She thanked God for her family;
she knew she had nothing to worry about.

In the phrase of the hymn:

"Hers was the sunlight; hers was the morning."

Her sunlight was the special sunlight of Northern Italy.
It never left her. She knew it in her childhood
and revelled in it in her young womanhood.

She was born on 29 December 1917 in Arzignano, Vicenza,
the daughter of a wine merchant, one of a family of nine children,
whose childhood seemed in retrospect to have been entirely *al fresco*.

For Laura especially, the call of the high hills was irresistible.
Look up at the gaunt crags of the Dolomites and you see creation
at its most awesome; but look down from those mountain heights
to the valleys below and you see the world at its loveliest.

She loved it. She became a founder-member of the Alpine
Association. She adored skiing and the sunlight on the snow.
In her last months she showed me a beautiful book
of photographs of the Dolomites, the lakes and glaciers,
stunning in the mountain sunshine. And we also discovered
that we were both fans of that atmospheric 1948 film
The Legend of the Glass Mountain – the music from it
will be my tribute to her as she leaves the church.

But don't imagine Laura as a Dulcie Gray or Julie Andrews figure.

Laura was tough, and needed to be tough. When war broke out in 1939 she was twenty-two, and engaged.
But the man whom she loved was killed at Tobruk, which Rommel captured in 1942, and Laura's private world collapsed. She could never love anyone else again.

It freed her, in the event, to give all her energies and strength to the resistance. When Mussolini's empire collapsed in July 1943, Northern Italy found itself under Nazi rule. The resistance united white- and blue-collar workers, and peasants, against a common enemy.

The war in the mountains needed many small groups, sometimes socialist, sometimes Catholic – the Green Flames. They needed people like Laura who knew the mountains and yet seemed harmless. She learned how to pick pockets, how to suss out information. She was able to carry grenades in a suitcase. She could smuggle passes and weapons to those who needed them.

The whole family lived dangerously – sheltering a family of South African Jews in their loft, while entertaining the occupying forces downstairs. On one occasion she was tipped off by a friendly German soldier and missed a firing squad by five minutes.

Tragically, at the end of 1944, General Alexander announced a suspension of operations for the winter – a tactical blunder which enabled the Nazis to unleash a terrible offensive against the resistance. Some 40,000 of them died. But those sacrifices were not in vain. Fascism came to an end and Italy regained its freedom. And so did Laura.

One day a cousin was leaving and they asked a couple of passing British soldiers to take a snap. As there was only one more left on the roll, Laura offered to take a photo of the two soldiers. And she told them where to come to collect it when it was developed. Laura's maid was the chaperone necessary for such

an encounter, but Laura won the day by telling the maid:
"Say your rosary; back soon!"

Those rosaries worked awfully well. Alec Cunningham,
who had also vowed never to marry after the end of a relationship,
fell in love with her. Laura was cautious: "Go home; try to forget me;
wait six months, and if you feel the same then, come back in civvies."

Laura and Alec were married on 8 June 1946 (the feast of
St William of York) and spent their honeymoon on Lake Garda.
And then she came to England and buckled down to working-class
life, and power cuts, and ration books. Hard to imagine the change
in her life-style, but she just got on with it.

At first they lived with the in-laws in Fulham.
Their only daughter, Catherine, was born on 24 June 1947,
and in 1950 they came to Edgware. Alec flourished as a paper
merchant and Laura became fluent in a dialect all her own.
She was a dedicated wife and mother and a tremendous
neighbour and friend.

Eventually Catherine married Dinos, when the Cunninghams
followed the Woolfs to Marsh Lane, where Laura lived
happily ever after.

And I mean that, because even when the spinal stenosis
seemed to cramp her life so much, her serenity was an act
of will. She would make the best of any situation. Alec died
in December 1994 so she had six years of active widowhood.
It was then that she joined the SVP here, brilliant especially
at visiting, both the housebound and people at Woodland Hall.
Then she became housebound herself.

Almost as soon as I arrived here, I began to visit her with
Communion. She asked if I'd mind if she said the *Confiteor*
in Italian, and I said of course she could, and why not the
Our Father as well. It brought Italy into our meetings
and conversations, and let the sunshine in.

She was a wise and tolerant lady who thought that
if a thing was worth doing, it was worth doing well.
Even from a wheelchair she would pour coffee with
the regal air of the natural hostess.

And she never looked anything but well-groomed.
It's one of those consoling facts that just before she died
she was waiting to come home from hospital and had
her hair done. She didn't die bedraggled, but ready to
return home and resume her natural place as Queen Bee.

It was my privilege to know her and to admire her
unfeignedly. A brave and courageous woman,
independent, loving, compassionate, original –
and such fun. And especially to see how she
epitomised the love and strength that means family.

She absolutely adored her grandchildren. It was wonderful
to have a grand-daughter in Italy, and she couldn't wait to
show me the photos of Christian and Vicky's wedding.
You think your wedding day is the happiest day of your
life, she said. And then later you realise that the happiest
day is when you see your child get married. And when
you're old, it's the happiest day of all to be at the
wedding of your grandchild.

I'm so glad she lived to see that day – it was the summit of
her life's mountain and the view from the top was breathtaking.

Following St Paul's advice to the Philippians:

"All that is true, all that is noble, all that is just and pure, all that is lovable and gracious, whatever is excellent and admirable, fill all your thoughts with these things."

On a BBC Symphony Orchestra tour of Eastern Europe, a chance to see the Parliament Building in Budapest.

From left: Cormac Rigby, Heather Harper, Freda Grove (Concerts Organiser), (now Canon) Andrew Meynell of Victor Hochhauser Ltd., and our translator.

Chapter 11

So that the world may believe.

When I was a boy and went to bed I was allowed extra time
to read in bed. I was trusted not to exceed five to ten minutes
to get to the end of my chapter, and then as I switched off the light,
I'd call downstairs, "G'night and God bless."
And Mother would call back "G'night and God bless."

Years later, in the sixties when I was closing down the Home
Service after the shipping forecast, I'd say something on similar lines:
"For all of us on duty here in Broadcasting House this is
Cormac Rigby wishing you Good night and God bless."

That phrase was queried one morning by my boss, himself
a Catholic incidentally. "Do you think it's right", he said,
"to invoke the deity in that way? After all, not all listeners
are believers."

"Of course not", I said, "But *I* am. You're instructing me
to sign off personally by name, not as the anonymous
voice of the Corporation but as a named announcer
and when Cormac Rigby says 'Good night' he always
says 'Good night and God bless'."

My boss thought about it and said,
"Fair enough. If it's what you normally and naturally say, carry on."

That was quite a significant conversation. It made a very
important distinction between what the BBC would say
and what a named presenter would say. The BBC was
very cautious in those days – and rightly so – about the
cult of personality. Programmes mattered, presenters didn't.

For a long time newsreaders were totally anonymous.
The practice of naming them began during the war to help

listeners tell the difference between the caricature voice of
the Nazi propagandist William Joyce, "Lord Haw-Haw",
and the genuine voices of such newsreaders as John Snagge,
Alvar Liddell, Wilfred Pickles and Frank Phillips. When Frank
Phillips retired in 1965, I was his replacement on the BBC staff.

Reading the news was not a personality thing. The newsreaders
were named but their job was above controversy and personality.
And indeed throughout my fourteen years as chief announcer
on Radio 3, I would never allow Radio Times to publish photos
of the announcers. It didn't matter what we looked like;
it was what we said that mattered.

In those still Reithian days, the newsreaders were not allowed
to do anything that might compromise the integrity of the news.

So when I began in my spare time to review ballet performances
for the press I was not allowed to use my own name for what
might be construed as controversial writing. I had to adopt
a *nom de plume*. When my pieces appeared in the *Oxford Mail*
or *The Times* or *Dance and Dancers*, I wrote as John Cowan.
It seems, in retrospect, a very austere policy, but its purpose
was to keep the news uncontaminated.

Times changed. The television newsreader Angela Rippon
did a high-kicking dance routine with Morecambe and Wise
and nowadays newsreaders are quite likely to have theatrical agents
negotiating their salaries. That's an inevitable consequence of going
from a corporate voice to personalities. We no longer think of a
newsreader as a voice of objectivity. The individual stands on his
or her own and they survive as broadcasters for as long as they
pull in the listeners. Some come and go without any impact.
Others – like Jimmy Young, or Terry Wogan or Richard Baker –
seem to have the secret of eternal life already.

I still get letters, sixteen years after leaving the BBC,
referring to things I said on air –
and not least that "Good night and God bless" at close-down.

Such things have value. Being a Catholic on Radio 3 didn't mean reading the news in Latin or playing *God bless the Pope* instead of *God save the Queen.* It simply meant following Paul's advice to the Philippians:

> And now my friends all that is true, all that is noble,
> all that is just and pure, all that is lovable and gracious,
> whatever is excellent and admirable fill all your thoughts
> with these things.

No medium is more revealing than radio.
Insincerity, phoniness, is immediately apparent:
you can hear in the words how the mind is orientated.
Thoughts that are full of the goodness of God become
easily discernible.

Being a Catholic isn't a label; it's a key part of the personality.
And it is very important that such personalities should be at work
in the media: radio, TV and press.

I'm not too fussed about having overtly Christian radio stations –
by and large they preach to the converted. I'm much more concerned
that in all areas of the media there are personalities reflecting love of
God and Christian values, that in the normal processes of the media
there are good Catholics who are also highly competent broadcasters
and journalists: I don't mean clergy in God slots, but professional
laymen everywhere. Such people are literally a Godsend.
The world of the media is where Christians are needed
so that the world may believe.

For most of my working life, the Sunday after Ascension has been
designated Communications Sunday. How should we mark it?
First, by praying for any good person who needs real moral
courage and spiritual strength to work in that industry.
And second, supporting training and familiarisation processes
which empower Christian leaders, Christian lay people,
to have the communication skills to make an impact.

Politics sets great store by training spin-doctors for the media. The Church sets great store by training its own members to reflect the love of God in the media.

The effectiveness of the message is often determined by the personality of the communicator.

Chapter 12

He was angry then, and refused to go in.

We've heard this story of the Prodigal Son too often.
We know it too well.

Don't you think the elder son had a point? He'd been absolutely
loyal to his father all the time; he'd done everything asked of him,
"slaved for you and never once disobeyed your orders."
And then he sees the father caving in to the unreasonable
demands of baby brother.

The older boy had long accepted that one day, when the old man
died, the property would be divided equally between both his sons.
But he's outraged when the younger one demands to anticipate
that dividing-up and to have his half now. Suddenly the estate is
only half what it used to be – and he's got to keep slaving in the
half that remains – not nearly as cost-effective, not nearly as easy
to manage. So while Junior goes gallivanting in foreign parts,
squandering his inheritance, the older brother is left struggling
to make half an estate work reasonably well.

Then – well we've heard the story many times – we know
the wanderer got his comeuppance. He lost his money to
false friends and ended up on the scrap-heap. Whereupon
the penny dropped that he'd be better off at home and he
came crawling back, sadder but wiser. *Ah, bless him!*

The old man is overwhelmed, sees him coming, runs out
to meet him, orders a feast. Now is that fair? Is that justice?

It's all very well forgiving the young lad for being such a fool,
but is it fair on the older brother? The fatted calf is killed –
and that of course comes from his half of the estate.
And a robe, and sandals, and a ring are provided,
and of course they come from the older brother's half too.

It's very easy for the father to forgive the prodigal son.
He'd always been indulgent to him and the homecoming
is very emotional. The boy comes back home crestfallen
and terribly thin. And the father finds forgiveness
welling up inside him.

And of course the boy knows just how to play it:
I really am sorry, Dad. I've been a complete idiot.
I've sinned against heaven and you. I'm not worthy to be your son.
Ah, bless him!

And that easy return is followed by easy forgiveness.
The boy is happy, the father is happy.

Only the older son is unconvinced. That Jackanapes only
has to flutter his eyelashes and everyone's welcoming him home.
What about me? I'm just not appreciated round here.

Forgiveness is very easy if

> you haven't been really damaged,
> the culprit grovels suitably, and
> emotion is uppermost.

It's not so easy if

> you've been taken for granted,
> the culprit ignores you, and
> it's not a spontaneous reaction of the heart,
> but an act of will

We don't know from the Gospel what finally happened.
We hear the father being all statesmanlike and generous and
indulgent: "Your brother here was dead and has come to life."
Ah, bless him!

It looks as though we're supposed to think that the brother
then found it as easy to forgive as it had been for the father.
Well, it wasn't.

And this is the real message of the Gospel.

Forgiveness only matters when it's NOT easy.

The more I read the parable, the more I think the hero
is not the father who was indulgent to give him the money
in the first place and who was easily moved to forgiveness
when he came back.

No, I think the real hero is the older son who'd been exploited
and ignored and for whom forgiveness wasn't a sloppy knee-jerk
reaction. He had to get over his resentment, subdue his sense
of unfairness, make allowances for immaturity, and forget his
justifiable sense of injustice. For him to think his way through
all that and then be prepared to join in the welcome –
that was quite something.

Often we find that forgiveness is easy enough.
The challenge comes when we've been seriously wronged
and have to ignore our natural reactions and choose to forgive.

Forgiveness isn't an act of indulgence – *Ah, bless him!*
Forgiveness is an exercise of the will to go beyond fairness and justice.

For the man of property, glad to have his boy home again,
forgiveness was pretty easy.

For the older brother, forgiveness was genuinely heroic.

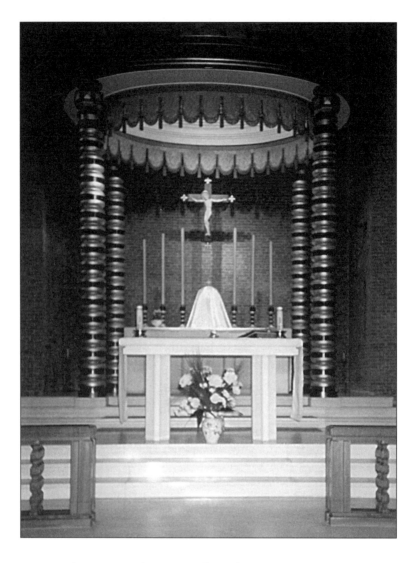

*The new stone altar in St William of York, Stanmore, is based
on the design of the altars in the side-chapels by the original architect,
Hector Corfiato. It was made and donated by Jim Keegan of the Marble Studio.*

Chapter 13

This is my body which will be given up for you.

Friday evening brought me my happiest moments since
I came to Stanmore. It was the feast of our revered patron
St William of York, and we were able to mark the occasion
by using for the first time our beautiful new stone altar.

Forty years ago, our architect created an impact of clear
priorities. As you came into the church your eye travelled up
the sanctuary steps to the altar, the tabernacle and the crucifix.
The crucified Jesus looked down on the altar where the
Sacrifice of the Mass was offered.

"The perfect sacrifice . . . that Christ offered on the Cross
as a total offering to the Father's love and for our salvation.
By uniting ourselves with his sacrifice, we can make
our lives a sacrifice to God."

The Mass is precisely that: Jesus enabling us to unite ourselves
to his sacrifice as he offers his life to the Father.

That original layout of the church was how I remember all the
churches of my boyhood. But in the years after Vatican II,
altars were brought forward so that the priest and people gather
round them and the people can see clearly what is going on.

Catholic churches all over the world had to rethink the position
of the altar. In Stanmore it was impossible to move the high altar
and there was no room to slot the celebrant in behind it.
So a temporary solution was tried: a moveable wooden structure
on wheels was placed at the top of the first sanctuary steps
so that there the priest could say Mass facing the people.
It served the purpose well. But for far too long.

Twenty years ago, Bishop Harvey said he wanted to see us have
a permanent stone altar so the priest could face the people at Mass.

Fr Finnegan briefed an architect to examine how that might
be done. There were two possibilities. First, to move the
old high altar four feet forward to the front of the baldachino.
Or, more radically, to dismantle the baldachino and remove the
steps leading up to it and then resite the high altar at the lower
level, well forward of its present position, and then erect a
mensa and tabernacle against the back wall.

In February 1983 a meeting was called to discuss those proposals.
But it was clear that the cost would be enormous,
that there'd be much disruption and – most significantly
of all – that the present architectural beauty and integrity
of the sanctuary would be destroyed.

Fortunately, those big schemes were put on hold and the
temporary meals-on-wheels altar continued to serve.
Unfortunately, the temporary altar was both solid enough
to block the sightlines and insubstantial enough to look makeshift.
Its cobbled-together physical appearance sat uneasily beside
the high quality of all the other woodwork in the church.
It was not a worthy centrepiece for the liturgy of the Eucharist.
And so it became my burning desire to find a solution for the
problem and to create an altar worthy of the Sacrifice.

In 1983 Dennis Allman had written to Fr Finnegan strongly
resisting the huge scheme of demolition and suggesting instead
that the old high altar and the baldachino be left as they are
(as a focal point for the Real Presence) and that a simple stone altar
– perhaps just two uprights supporting a stone table top –
be erected where the wooden altar is now sited.

That solution would fulfil the bishop's directive to have a
permanent stone altar allowing the priest to face the congregation
when celebrating Mass. It would cause no disruption and above all
the essential characteristics of the architectural design of the sanctuary
would be maintained.

That solution seemed to me eminently sensible and I've given much thought and effort to implement it. I looked at redundant altars in other churches and chapels but none suited. It struck me that if we modelled our new altar on the altars in the side chapels, we would be in close harmony with the original architect's thinking.

I described what I had in mind to the parish council and, to my great delight, the council providentially included a parishioner able to translate a dream into reality. I'm profoundly grateful to Jim Keegan who took the idea and ran with it and created an altar which at long last is worthy of its function. Marvellous that it could be used for the first time on the feast of St William of York.

Does it really matter so much? – Oh yes.

When the Sacrifice of the Mass came under attack at the time of the Reformation there took place the "stripping of the altars" – the altars were ripped out of churches and cathedrals and replaced by wooden tables so that Communion would be seen as no more than a ritual meal rather than in its true significance as the Holy Sacrifice of the Mass. The stone altar is the symbol of the sacrifice.

At the Last Supper, Christ took the bread and said,
"This is my body which will be given up for you."
On Calvary he offered up that Body in sacrifice,
a sacrifice infinitely transcending all man's sacrifices.

During the Mass, we tune in to that eternal sacrifice which is the ultimate expression of love, the love of the Redeemer Son for the Creator Father.

As the Council of Trent defined it: "In this divine sacrifice which is celebrated in the Mass, the same Christ who offered himself once in a bloody manner on the altar of the Cross is contained, and is offered in an unbloody manner."

We are the creatures for whom Christ's sacrifice was made and so the altar of his sacrifice is most precious in our eyes.

Blessed John XXIII, who wanted to let fresh air into the Church. On this 1959 Vatican City stamp, Pope John venerates the remains of his predecessor both as Patriarch of Venice and Bishop of Rome, Saint Pius X.

Chapter 14

You worry and fret about so many things,
and yet few are needed, indeed only one.

One of the things Catholics sometimes worry and fret about is modernising, updating, keeping up to date. Yet only one requirement is paramount – that we should love God and our neighbour as ourselves.

I remember Pope John XXIII, Blessed Pope John, saying that he wanted to open the windows and let some fresh air in – and the next thing was a small army of militant Marthas not just *opening* windows, but knocking windows out – and altars too – and letting in not just fresh air but every secular gale that was blowing.

Now don't get me wrong: this isn't a tirade against progress or a lament for the Guild of St Agnes or a plea for the restoration of maniples. I actually believe that each generation needs to bring its own insights into the spiritual life of the Church.

The true growth of the Church is revealed in the history of its saints – it's the growth and development of holiness down through the centuries that is the real history of the Church. Never lose sight of that – what matters is not modernising but consistency in holiness.

When I was in Ireland earlier this month I spent some time in the little town in Leitrim where my grandfather was born, and where my mother was always at her happiest. That area around Drumshanbo I've known for years. I was taken out for dinner one evening by friends in Drumshanbo; we took a familiar road out of the town, heading out past what used to be a station house in the old days of the narrow-gauge railway, which used to run alongside and sometimes across the road. The track was taken up years since but the little house survives, refurbished. Then we turned right towards where cousins lived in Drumbollog and beyond to a village called Kiltubrid.

Now the Irish are very strange in their use of names. My grandfather went to Mass in Drumshanbo – but the official name of the parish is Murhaun. And when you go into the church at Kiltubrid you find the parish is called Drumcong.

I remembered the original rather damp and dull old church, typical of its kind but neglected. And then the worrying and fretting began. They decided the old church had had its day and they wanted something modern and exciting.

I remember going out with my mother to see this eighth wonder of the Leitrim world. Much of it looked prefabricated. There was a huge amount of glass which turned it into an outsize greenhouse when it was sunny – and which must have felt bleaker than bleak when it drizzled. In summer it was stifling and full of bluebottles buzzing against all those windows.

We thought it was much over-rated. In fact – let's be honest – we thought it was simply horrid, soulless and dull. And – this is the interesting bit – so did the people of the parish. They didn't like its sweltering hotness in summer or its cold draughtiness in winter.

A new priest came along and heard what the people were saying. And he made the bold decision to abandon the smart new church and turn back to the old one. By then it was pretty decrepit, but the parishioners took it in hand and lovingly and carefully restored it.

They reset the lovely colourful Victorian stained glass and complemented it with new glass. They put in under-floor heating and then a fine new stone floor. The traditional old wooden benches were still there, and they smartened them up

so they look both solid and lovely. Best of all they reordered
the sanctuary, bringing the altar forward – a specially made
altar and presidential chair matching the shrine behind them
to house the Blessed Sacrament. The crowning grace was to
clad the entire ceiling in timber – which looked terrific and
did marvels for the acoustic.

I could hardly believe it. The old church had only needed
cherishing and affection – it proved more than capable
of restoration. It's not just restored; it's relaunched.
It's beautiful; it's prayerful; it speaks of love and service.
And the awful monstrosity on the other side of the road
has now been sold to developers.

I was struck by the truth it proclaimed. The worrying and
fretting to build for the sake of modernity is wasted energy;
all it erected was a costly and inappropriate white elephant.
What was needed was love of God and neighbour –
the willingness to give love and practical expression in the
old building so that it came to life again. When I reflect
on the history of the Church – or indeed the state of the
contemporary Church, the Kiltubrid experience seems
very eloquent.

It's a delusion to think that throwing money at a swanky
modern church is the same as creating a home for God.
What creates God's house is the genuine love and practical service
of those who spiritually live there. It's not modernising that
is the key to development but whole-hearted holiness.

What I'm saying is: beware of those who worry and fret
about modernising. Their solution is to abandon old
structures, time-tested devotions, familiar customs.
The real solution is to concentrate instead on the beauty
of holiness, the courage of the apostles, the determination
of the desert fathers, the ingenuity of the friars and mendicants,
the dedication of the new orders – Jesuits, Redemptorists,

and so on, the gentle work of the teaching and nursing orders,
the enthusiasm of today's new movements; all these
build the Church on love.

Modernising for the sake of keeping up with the secular Joneses
is a foolish pursuit – it terminates in modernism and spiritual
bankruptcy. But to refresh and renew the Church is the way
of organic growth and fresh impetus to the world of the Spirit.

"You worry and fret about so many things,
and yet few are needed – indeed only one."

"All you need is love."

Chapter 15

Yourselves turned outside.

That's the fear that lurks at the back of our mind when life ends,
and we approach the gates of eternity: will we be allowed in –
or not?

We console ourselves first of all with the solemn assurance
that God takes no pleasure in the death of the wicked –
that he wants all to come to repentance.

So we say to ourselves, well – at least the judge isn't biased
against us. He's a loving Father, he's merciful and forgiving.
And that's fine: we'll get a fair trial.

And then conscience pricks us, and we wonder do we *deserve*
to be acquitted? It's not what we've done but why we've done it
that matters. Check list out: Sunday Mass, yes.
Prayers – yes, especially when there's a panic on.
Faith – wobbly at times. Love? Friendliness?
Real acts of genuine love of people?
The unseen, unknown acts of kindness –
are they plentiful in our lives or collector's items?
Do my talents serve my vanity or serve others?
Do I waste my time, or spend it wisely?
These are the questions that niggle.

If I don't go to Mass on Sunday, is it a sin? Now there's a question!
Straight answer: yes. The duty laid on us by the Precepts of the
Church is that "You shall attend Mass on Sundays and holydays
of obligation."

And as soon as you give a straight answer, in come the barrack-room
lawyers: But what if I'm over sixty? What if I'm on holiday in a
Muslim country? What if I honestly forgot?

What if I get to the church and there's no Mass?

You see at once we've started treating the whole thing
as if it were the small print on a contract.

When someone asks me if you're bound to go to Mass
on Sunday, I ask if you're bound to kiss your lover? If you're
spending all your mental energy trying to talk your way out
of basic obligations, then your heart isn't in it – and if your
heart isn't in it, your physical presence isn't worth much.

That was the mistake the Pharisees made. They worked out
an elaborate code of practice and they lost sight of God.
Their God was not love. Their God was a Code of Behaviour.

What is our faith? We believe that God created us so he
could give us existence and love us, not just here but forever.
We believe that the gift of free will has been a gift much
abused and that we damage ourselves and others horribly.
We believe that to rescue us the God who loves us
sent his Son to show us what Love is really like.

His life on earth, his death on the Cross, his rising from
the dead are actions that invite us to fall head over heels
in love with him.

I don't love Our Lord because that's the rule.
I love him because his love for me is greater than anyone
else's could possibly be. I love him, not because I have to,
but because I long to.

The Mass is where we meet him – at the Last Supper,
on Calvary, risen from the dead. We are alongside him
as he offers himself for us.

And so coming to Mass isn't a duty, an obligation,
it's a privilege, and a delight, and I can't get enough of it.

Does he really only insist on a visit once a week?
Surely he welcomes us every day and opens up his heart to us?

And in his presence, I open my heart to him.

There aren't many people I can really open my heart to.
How lucky I am that one of them is the Son of God.

Being saved isn't a matter of ticking off duties on a checklist
but entering the door into my best friend's house. It's one of the
happiest feelings in life: arriving on the doorstep of your best friend's
house and ringing the bell and waiting for the door to be opened.
That's heaven. And it would be hell to be turned away.

But what sort of a door is it? Well actually it's my sort of door,
my size, my shape. It's a narrow door, yes. My own door,
and I have my own key. And all I have to do is use them.

Lots of people ignore their own door. They want to go with
the crowd, flock to the party, follow the buzz – go where false
friends hang out. Everybody welcome. Just bring your Self.

Imagine. They have their own door and they throw away the key.
And the one good friend they've got waits in vain for them.
Too late they realise their mistake. The key of love isn't needed
because the whole scene is lots of selfs milling around.
They get lots of excitement, lots of money, lots of possessions
but nobody loves them.

And when the music stops and the balloons burst and their
beauty fades and their brains crumble; they're only an empty self
and they die alone.

The door we need the key to
is the door of Love, and the key to it is giving ourselves –
loving people as Jesus loved people. The more you shape yourself
to Jesus, the more the door of love opens to you.

And that's why I love the Mass. It's the point in each day
where I can shape myself to Jesus.

In Memoriam.

—✠—

EDWARD THRING,

Born	Came to Uppingham	Died
NOV. 29th, 1821.	SEPT. 10th, 1853.	OCT. 22nd, 1887.

—✠—

" He giveth His beloved sleep."

A T length the strenuous heart is still,
  At last the brain from thought may cease ;
Strong worker of the Father's will,
  A son of GOD, he enters peace.

He rests, in solemn silence laid ;
  We leave him wrapt in slumber deep ;
Our hymns shall sound, our prayers be said,
  And weave a charm about his sleep.

His lips are hushed, but every stone
  In this fair pile his faith had raised
Shall speak his clear familiar tone ;
  Wrong shall be scorned and right be praised.

False thoughts, false deeds, shall never mar
  The joy of his eternal rest ;
For he is near, though he is far,
  His guardian spirit is our guest.

Oh ! Lord of Love, and Life, and Truth,
  Break Thou the dark sepulchral seal ;
Be Head, be Master, of our youth,
  And unto each Thyself reveal.

H. D. R.

Sung in UPPINGHAM SCHOOL CHAPEL, *October 27th,* 1887.

A Victorian memory card.
"Keeping people's names fresh,
keeping people in the sight of God."

I will not let you die, Edward Thring,
born 1821 died 22 October 1887
strenuous worker
discovering and developing
the unique talent in every boy.

Chapter 16

Hurry, because I must stay at your house today.

The story of Zacchaeus is one of the most encouraging in the whole of the Bible. He lived in Jericho and he wasn't short of a bob or two. But he was short of an inch or two – definitely the Wayne Sleep of Jericho – small and full of energy.

When he heard that Jesus was coming, he realised he wouldn't be able to see him unless he commandeered some vantage point. So he ran on ahead – I told you he was full of energy – and scrambled up a sycamore tree, and from there he could see Jesus and the crowds milling around him.

And to his amazement, Jesus looked up – and he didn't say "Hey, you", he actually knew his name. Someone must have briefed him that if he saw a small but perfectly-formed little man in rich clothes making frantic efforts to see him, it would be Zacchaeus. So Jesus calls up to him by name, "Zacchaeus, come down and hurry up, because I'm coming to stay at your place today."

Zacchaeus could hardly contain himself. He bounced down and danced along in front of Jesus to show him the way to his house. And of course there were loads of grumbles from the religious crowd: typical Nazareth sort of thing to do: ignore the respectable and go off hob-nobbing with the tax-collectors.

But Zacchaeus refused to be put out. He said to Jesus, very bravely: "I'm really glad you've come. I've not exactly led a perfect life – lots of dosh and a nice house, but I know perfectly well that some of my wealth wasn't exactly honestly earned. But this is the moment when I can turn my life around and make amends. I'm going to give half of all I've got to the poor, and if I've swindled anyone, I'll pay him back fourfold."

And Jesus said: "Well done, my friend; you're just the sort of fellow I've come to seek out. The smug and the self-righteous can carry on congratulating themselves – but from today you can enjoy a good conscience and a generous heart. You're a son of Abraham too – and my brother – and I'm the Son of Man and you're my brother; and I'm so glad I've found you and given you a fresh start."

Jesus could so easily have passed by – but no,
he went out of his way to rescue Zacchaeus.
"I will not let you die, Zacchaeus."

And that perception of what Jesus wants to do comes very well at the beginning of November, the month of the Holy Souls. Why do we remember them? Because they stand in need of forgiveness and we can help by praying for them. Of course Jesus can forgive them – all of them, without our intervention. But that's not his way. He claims brotherhood with us. He wants to involve us in his work of salvation. He knows us by name – just as he knew Zacchaeus. He says: Don't just stand there, goggling at me – do something – make me welcome, give me a drink – help me in my work.

And we say, How Lord: how can we help you?
By preaching? Yes, of course.
By good example? Yes, of course; and by praying.
Praying? Yes, praying.
Keeping people in your thoughts and prayers,
keeping people's names fresh,
keeping people in the sight of God.

Of course, God can do perfectly well without our help.
But when we put our minds to helping his work we are
not only helping him, we are helping ourselves.

And so we think, we think prayerfully, of those like ourselves,
weak mortals, whose assets weren't always honestly earned
and who have suddenly had to face God.

Never does anyone stand so terribly alone as at the moment
of death, when all the mistakes, the errors, the sins, look so
terribly stacked against us in the bright glare of God's truth.

It's Purgatory. And there is nothing we can do to help ourselves.
But we are sustained by the prayers of others, helping us in
our shame, interceding for us, propping us up with their love.

At that moment we might well wish that the earth would open
and swallow us up and extinguish us altogether. But then we
hear the voices raised on our behalf making excuses for us,
giving explanations, but above all simply saying,
"We loved her; we loved him. For the sake of our love,
forgive her, forgive him, and draw her, draw him
through this purging into the light of eternal bliss."

It is our determination to help that matters.
Our determination not to let these souls seem loveless and alone.
Our determination not to let them die for ever,
but to remember them and pray them into paradise.

Our November prayers for the Holy Souls are the acts
of loving remembrance which God loves to accept
as the trigger of his mercy.

The American poet Sam Ambler wrote a wonderful poem
which refuses to let people die in anonymity, but to name them,
as Jesus named Zacchaeus.

It is a strategy of love. Each three-line verse consists of
the clause "I will not let you die", followed by the name of
the individual; a second line bears the birth and death dates
of that individual, and a third line, slightly more expansive,

briefly highlights a unique contribution made by that person
to the good of the world.

For example:

> I will not let you die, Michael Calvert
> born 1958 died January 1987
> crafting floral epithets into bouquets
> of people poems
> for AIDS commiseration.

The accumulation of names and lives takes on the character
of a formal act of remembrance, a litany of ordinary saints.

It is a good practice.
It's not enough just to remember 'the Dead'.
There is a clear human need to remember them *by name*,
as every War Memorial in the land testifies.

It is a natural human inclination to cherish a memory,
a specific memory, of particular individuals.
Every photo on our mantelpieces testifies to that.

It is natural for humans to try to keep alive the memory
of those who have been loved and admired:

> "John Brown's body lies a-mouldering in the grave,
>   but his soul goes marching on."

It is a strategy of human love not to let people die,
but to keep them ever-present, as the Victorian memory card
and the late twentieth-century poet try to do.

But beyond and above all that
is the Christian affirmation of the after-life:
it's not just the memory lingering on;
it is the real person who comes through the experience of death
into an eternal existence.

The mere keeping-alive of a memory
lasts only as long as memory itself lasts.

The remembrance of the Church,
its celebration of All Souls,
encourages us to remember by name
those who have died.
It is the proclamation of the communion of saints,
the proclaiming that death does not separate us,
and that the members of Christ's mystical body
continue to pray for each other:
the Church Militant joining its prayers
to those of the Church Triumphant
for the Holy Souls.

That is the idea that underlies the list of names we cherish
and remember in November.

> I will not let you die, Zacchaeus,
> born in 10 BC, died AD 45,
> spotting the Lord from a distance
> and opening your heart to prepare a welcome for him

> I will not let you die, John Eccles,
> born 1939, died January 1964,
> awakening life and love,
> bequeathing love and life,
> doubling my will to live and love.

"For we know we shall see our brother again
and enjoy his friendship."

"*Eternity is present to us, as Jesus in the Blessed Sacrament
gently but blazingly offers himself for us.*"

*This picture was a response to a sermon. Andrew Latham,
of Most Sacred Heart parish, gave it to Father Cormac.*

Chapter 17

There in their presence he was transfigured.

What an extraordinary happening it was –
the transfiguring of Jesus while those three apostles
watched him, overwhelmed with amazement.

There was the ordinary but remarkable Jesus they knew –
one in a million – but still a man like themselves, and suddenly
up there on the mountain his face shone like the sun, and
Moses and Elijah appeared and began to speak with him.

Suddenly, and for a few precious seconds of time,
eternity broke through before their startled eyes.
The eternal Son of the Father for a few moments
stood before them in all his glory.

We know that still to come was the horror of his arrest
and crucifixion. Still to come the heartbreak as they took
his body down from the cross and thought it must all have
been a delusion: all his talk of the Father – and the Father
hadn't stirred a finger to rescue him.

Still to come was that even wilder swing of the pendulum,
when Peter and John ran to the tomb and realised he had
risen from the dead. Still to come was the realisation that
the Father had not abandoned him after all – and that Jesus
wished to offer his life on the Cross, a sacrifice, self-sacrifice:
the completest expression of love ever made.

The transfiguration was no illusion – it was the harbinger
of the truth, the first glimpse of the glory of the Risen Christ.

I'd like you to think for a few moments of the difference
between the cinema and the theatre. Very different experiences.

I don't often go to the cinema – I like films and admire them, but I'm saving them up for a rainy day. I'll watch films and videos when I can't get to live theatre any more.

In the cinema I see what clever and talented people did months and years ago – and one can re-run it and re-run it and it will always be the same: wonderful, inspiring, moving but unchanging and unchangeable. The same creation over and over again.

But in the theatre, though the words and the moves are set, the performance will always be different because it's going on now, in front of my eyes. It's not a recording, it's now.

On Tuesday I saw the final performance of the current season of Shakespeare's *King John*. It's been an enricher, an eye-opener; I've seen more in it each time I've been – and that was its very last performance. The cast disperses; it seems like I have only the visual memory, the mental video in my mind's eye – but there's also the way it has altered me – changed my perceptions and my understanding.

The live theatre happening now is an altogether different experience from the film which happened some time ago. The film is in essence *yesterday*. The play is in essence *today*. Hold that distinction for a few moments.

When Christians gather round the table and re-run the Last Supper and repeat the words and do it as a commemoration, it is like the film. It takes an historic event, 2000 years ago, and repeats it. And that is good.

But it's not all. That historic event itself was the entry into time of an eternal action. At the Last Supper, Christ offered himself to the Father for us, and in that dramatic moment he pinpointed his sacrifice of himself.

The love in his heart was made visible in his action:
This is my body which will be given up for you.

In a way then, the Mass is like a film because it is a frequent re-run
of an actual historical event. But it is so much more than that.
The Last Supper showed Christ, the Son of God, offering himself
to the Father. And that act of self-sacrificing love is going on now,
has always been going on, will always be going on: it is happening
now in the eternal Present. The Son is *now* offering himself
in sacrifice to the Father – and we see it in the Mass.

The Mass is not just a re-run of an old film; it's switching in
to the live theatre of love; it's tapping in to the energy of love
within the Trinity.

The Mass is live. Here, at Mass, we are made present
to the love of God within the Trinity.

The film angle is the re-enactment of a meal long ago;
the play angle is the live event, here and now, in the eternal present.

The Mass is not a video, made long ago, and played over and over.
The Mass brings us into the presence of the living live love of
the Son for the Father, offering himself in sacrifice.

Just as eternity was glimpsed by the apostles when Jesus
was transfigured, so eternity is present to us, as Jesus in the
Blessed Sacrament gently but blazingly offers himself for us.

It's not a dead event, caught on film. It's a living sacrifice,
before our very eyes. It's not a re-run; it's live.

In the fourth Eucharistic Prayer, we proclaim it. First the film:

> "Father we now celebrate this memorial of our redemption.
> We recall Christ's death, his descent among the dead,
> his resurrection, and his ascension to your right hand
> and looking forward to his coming in glory" –

We switch at this point from the film of past events
to the live theatre happening now.

"We offer you his body and blood, the acceptable
sacrifice which brings salvation to the whole world."

Not *brought* it, as Calvary, the film event, brought it,
but *brings* it, now, live,
because here and now Jesus
is loving the Father
with that self-consuming love,
a living sacrifice of praise.

The Mass is not a meal, not a replay.
It is the living sacrifice,
the present and eternal love of the Son for the Father.
The Blessed Sacrifice of the Mass
is like that moment of transfiguration:
for a few precious seconds of time
we participate in the eternal event
of Father, Son and Holy Spirit.

Chapter 18

Give peace, Lord, to those who wait for you.
(preached 14 and 15 September 2001 in the
immediate aftermath of the terrorist attacks)

The first and most important response to the atrocities
we have seen this week is to weep for the victims.

This is above all a human tragedy of unbearable proportions.
Most of those who died so violently and so horribly were not
combatants. They were people like you and me. They went
in to work as usual and they never came home again.

There were some who never knew what hit them.
But there were many who stared horror and death in the face.
I don't even want to try to imagine the circumstances.
Among them were some who bravely tried to resist their
murderers, even knowing that they must still die themselves,
and I think that is heroic.

There were many who, when they realised how close
they were to death, thought of the ones they loved,
and were able to declare their love one last time.
There were many not directly involved – firemen,
police, medics – who died because they had gone to help.
All we can do is grieve for them and resolve to do all we can
to honour their memory by working for peace.

The temptation is to lash out in anger when what we need to do,
above all, is to *think*.

I suppose the first thought is this: If I saw death coming towards me,
whose name would be on my lips? Would there be fear or serenity
in my heart? Would I die well or badly?

Those who came through the blitz faced it; those who lived
in the trenches in the 1914–18 war lived on the brink of hell.

We know now that it is not confined to history –
it is present reality, we were foolish to think otherwise.

We are all in one way or another trapped by death.
And that's why we can identify so easily with those frantic figures
at the windows above the flames – to burn or to jump?
I pray God I may never have to face such a choice.

We *must* grieve for the victims; we must reflect on our own
vulnerability, and then we need to think beyond that again.
An act of such colossal evil is clearly totally and absolutely wrong;
it is morally indefensible – it is never ever right to kill
the innocent. Of course. Of course.

But *why* does such evil exist?
How can it be that bright intelligent human beings
like you and me become so morally warped
that they turn airliners into flame-throwers
and destroy their own lives in order to destroy others?

Why? It's not blood-lust. Thought went into it,
highly sophisticated thought, and we can't deal with the outcome
of that thinking until we understand the thinking itself.

Let me try one angle: all those who died in the Twin Towers
were innocent individuals – there can be no question of that:
innocent victims, for whom we grieve. But think for a moment,
not of the people who died, but of the building they worked in.

I've seen the horror of last Tuesday compared to the attack
on Pearl Harbour because it came out of a clear blue sky
and was a brutal and callous crime. I don't actually think
it's a very good comparison. Pearl Harbour was miles away and
the victims were almost all military. The Twin Towers were in
the heart of the city and the victims almost all non-combatants.

I think there's a more interesting comparison – though I haven't
seen it made anywhere. The fall of the Twin Towers, it seems
to me, invites comparison with the Fall of the Bastille.
The *ancien régime* in France controlled the Bastille – its security
was absolute and it stood as a symbol of the regime it protected.
The aristocracy and the monarchy believed the Bastille to be
impregnable. And suddenly it fell. Not to artillery bombardment,
but to a mob of *sans culottes* – the ragged, the poor, the oppressed.
They saw the Bastille as a bulwark of oppression – and when
the Bastille fell, the French Revolution secured its *moment de gloire*.
The French still celebrate Bastille Day;
it was a symbol, like the Berlin Wall.
And such symbols are both the pride of those who built them
and the demonised targets of those they oppress.

For us the Twin Towers were a tourist attraction,
a hyper-skyscraper, the ultimate gesture of affluence.
Anything you can build, I can build higher.
The assertion of everything that money can buy.
The glittering home of wealth beyond imagining.
But there are many in the world who see such luxury
as an affront to those who live in poverty.

As I said earlier, the victims of the atrocity were decent
ordinary people, just like us. But for many, the Manhattan skyline
is not a Wonder of the World, but an icon of economic oppression.
For many the Twin Towers were a Bastille. And that's why, as we
pray our way through the complexities of those horrendous hours
last Tuesday, we have to ask ourselves not just about the individuals
who died, but about the nature of the buildings they were in.

Some saw them as a workplace, graphically uniting people of
every nation – a statement of international trade and co-operation.
Others saw the Twin Towers as the statement of *Mammon über alles* –
and that's why they were targeted.

I make no judgment. I simply observe it, as an historian should. There are many people for whom the Fall of the Twin Towers was like the Fall of the Bastille.

I fear the consequences. The grapes of wrath can poison the whole world. Peace is not achieved by attacking men, but by attacking the cause of their grievances.

It was good to hear the battle-hymn of the Republic at St Paul's on Friday. That's the America we need to rediscover. Maybe the Twin Towers sent out the wrong signals to many outside America. Maybe we should rediscover Julia Ward Howe's vision of the Truth that marches on.

> In the beauty of the lilies Christ was born across the sea
> With a glory in his bosom that transfigures you and me.
> As He died to make men holy, let us die to make men free.

Let us weep, let us pray, let us think.

Chapter 19

There are many rooms in my Father's house.

When I was a small boy learning about Jesus, one of the things I discovered was that he'd lived a very long time ago, but the events of his life were still relevant to *my* life. He was God as well as man, so he could see what was coming – what hadn't happened yet.

He died to atone for our sins, *all* of our sins, and two thousand years ago he knew what *my* sins were going to be – and still he wanted to die for me.

Two thousand years ago he knew all about me and he could see me – stealing biscuits from the biscuit barrel. And it hurt him to see me because I was deliberately doing wrong. Maybe it's hard to grasp that an act of mine which took place so many years after his death on Calvary was still one of the things that pinned him to the cross. There is a very deep and profound truth in that. It speaks graphically of my own responsibility for my own deeds.

My mother used to say to me that the Crown of Thorns wasn't really plaited by the Roman soldiers. They were doing it on my behalf. The thorns in that crown are *my* sins. I do wrong. Deliberately. And I am adding a thorn to that terrible crown pressing on the head of Christ.

When I grew up, I realised it is true. The sufferings of Jesus were caused by the total sum of all sins – mine and yours, and everyone else's. And I have to accept my responsibility for my share of those sufferings. It's a graphic way of expressing the truth that Christ died for me. I helped put him on the cross – my sin is one of the thorns in his crown. I face up to the fact that my sins have consequences.

Childhood perceptions: my response was invariably "Why?"
But I found it easy to see that the Crown of Thorns wasn't really
plaited by the Roman soldiers – the thorns were my sins.

Everything I do impacts on other people's lives.
Even what seems to be a private sin has an impact sooner
or later. I'm not blaming the Romans, or the Jews for putting
Christ on the cross because I know I'm responsible too.
And I'm reflecting on that these last few days —
the days of the three London nail bombs.

I'm not a terrorist. I'm not a fascist.
So what is my responsibility?
Everything I do impacts on other people's lives.
For good or evil. I hurt people. I've made them angry.
I've damaged lives. I've got in the way of other people's happiness.
And these nail bombs demonstrate the point.

No, I'm not the man who blew up that Soho pub,
but what did destroy it was prejudice. The people targeted
were the gay minority. A few days earlier the targets were
the ethnic minority. And it's no good us lamenting the atrocity
if we're still in any way responsible for it. The fear, the prejudice
that actually detonated those bombs was created by an atmosphere,
a climate of opinion. When someone denigrates a minority,
speaks uncharitably, laughs nastily, that person is putting a nail
into that bomb just as directly as my childhood stealing put a
thorn into Christ's crown.

A few sinners detonate the bombs, but many of us pack them with
nails. Every sneer at a Paki, every 'joke' against blacks, every whisper
against the Jews, every innuendo against gays — all of them nails,
nails in a bomb, nails pinning Christ to his Cross.

Every time a good Christian forgets that there are many
rooms in God's house and laughs at, or belittles or demeans
a brother of Christ, it is Christ who suffers the blow.

As a child I accepted that I had added thorns to the crown
of thorns. As an adult I have to accept that I have provided
nails for bombs. May God forgive me for all my careless
and unguarded words, for all my destructive thoughts;

and may all Christians examine their consciences and resolve never to do or say – or even think – *anything* that can lead to such atrocities.

There *are* many rooms in our Father's house, enough for *all* minorities.

Chapter 20

If anyone declares himself for me in the presence of men,
I will declare myself for him in the presence of my Father in heaven.

Those words of Jesus explain to me exactly why I am so confident that Basil Hume is now safely in the presence of God.

It was his vocation to declare himself for Christ in every detail of his life – not just in his preaching and teaching, but in the way he preserved his monastic simplicity of life, in the courtesy he extended to everyone he met, in the laughter and good-humour that were always bubbling up around him.

He looked the part – the tall, slightly stooped figure, the firmness, the gravitas of a bishop who was deeply serious about the worship of God and who clearly refused to take himself too seriously.
 The Prime Minister found the right phrase:
"He was goodness personified".

The chairman of Churches Together in Ruislip expressed the view of many Christians in a letter of condolence to Fr Peter:
"We pray that his example and vision will continue, in God's strength, to lead the church's outreach."
And I've had several letters from non-Christian friends, sad because he was not just a church leader but a voice of sense and sanity in a mad and greedy world, a good man who seemed relevant to other good men.

One wrote to me:

> The world is too short of goodness
> not to mourn the passing of a great and good man.
> I find it hard to sleep with the images of Kosovo in my mind
> and wish the Cardinal had lived a good deal longer.

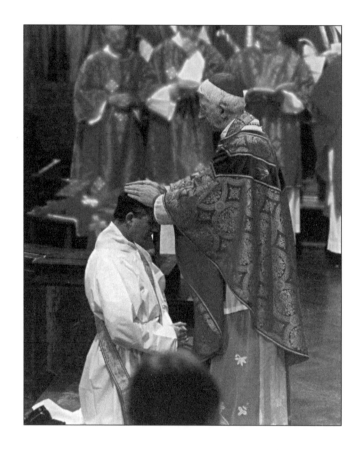

21 May 1988. Cardinal Basil Hume ordained
Father Cormac in Westminster Cathedral.

Photograph by Henry James.

We could all find fault with him in various ways, and he'd
be the first to find fault with himself. But he gradually came
to be recognised as an embodiment of recollected spirituality,
an awareness of the deepest value and significance of man.
A pointer to the mystery of the Cross and its overwhelming
meaning of love for sinful man. He had declared himself for
Christ in the presence of men and was aware that that was
his special mission.

On the face of it, it was an eccentric appointment. To bring
into the topmost place in the church in this country a man
who had no experience of life in a diocese, to take a man
who had deliberately chosen to anchor his life and his
priesthood in a Yorkshire abbey and to extricate him
from that stability and put him into the front line: madness!

But it showed that Rome actually understood the requirement.
The first three priorities at that stage were holiness, and holiness,
and holiness.

By being himself, by being what God had called him to do,
by being what the Holy Spirit had made him, Fr Basil became
the embodiment of what people truly wanted: the leadership
of a good man, a wise man and a man of prayer.

Today is Father's Day and any priest always feels a sense
of filial loyalty and affection towards his father in God, his bishop,
especially if it was that father who actually ordained him.
I remember vividly the impact he made on me at my ordination
and the impact he made on my friends from many backgrounds.

The tall silver-haired figure moved through the colourful
ceremonial with such natural dignity. He would have impressed
them if he'd never said a word! But his words were good too:
a homily on priesthood, and it was good to hear the laughter
that went round the cathedral when he noted wryly that I had
first gone off to a seminary – sent by Cardinal Godfrey to Rome –

in September 1961, but was only getting around to
being ordained by the next Cardinal but one in May 1988.
"Clearly", said the Cardinal, in his gently teasing way,
"Clearly God wanted you to have a very long formation".

When the time came for the gifts to be brought up
at the offertory by my family and closest friends,
my mother came first with the chalice she was giving me.
And she was very apprehensive. At eighty-four she was
okay going upstairs but not good at coming down stairs,
and she'd realised that there was no handrail to help her when
she turned away from the Cardinal to come down again.
But she needn't have worried. As he saw her approaching,
the Cardinal broke free from the Master of Ceremonies and
skipped down the stairs to meet her and the problem vanished.

Those two incidents of human sensitivity in the context of a
solemn ceremony were typical of the man. He had his mind
focussed on the transcendent God but that enabled him to
keep his eyes open to seeing God in those around him.

He was an integrated Christian, loving and loveable, holy
and warm, dignified but unstuffy. You were never in doubt
that he was in touch with God and therefore in touch with
God's creatures.

God had chosen him – as he thought – for a cloistered life,
and so he in turn chose the life of a monk. But in choosing
to put himself into the hands of God, he ended up not in the
place of his own choosing but where God wanted him to be.

God clearly wanted him to have a very long formation,
the formation that would enable him for the rest of his life
to declare himself for God in the presence of men.

May he rest in peace.

Chapter 21

He is not here, for he has risen as he said he would.

The authorities had put an armed guard over the tomb of Jesus
to guard against possible fraud. They dreaded the theft of the
corpse followed by an upsurge of rumours about rising from
the dead – as he had said he would.

They needn't have bothered as far as Jesus' disciples were concerned.
It was quite clear that the followers of Jesus had simply melted away –
far too scared and defeated to get up to any fraud.
They'd all disappeared when Jesus was brought to trial.
Even Peter, the brave and blustering Peter, three times
denied any involvement with Jesus.

Only the disciple whom Jesus loved, John, stayed with him
to the end, standing beneath the cross to give support to Mary.

When permission was given to take the body down from
the cross there were no apostles to do it, only the disciples
Joseph of Arimathea and Nicodemus, names deserving
to be remembered for their courage. And that was it.

On the Saturday, John was fully occupied looking after
the heartbroken Mother. Peter was close to despair –
it doesn't need much imagination to realise what Peter felt
when the cocks started crowing on the Saturday morning,
sending splinters of remorse into his heart.

The rest was silence. And the tomb was empty.
The lifeless body of Jesus lay there, but the spirit of Jesus
had left it with his last breath, and he was among the departed
in that barren land on the far shore of the river Styx
which some call Sheol, that state of existence to which
we refer in our creed as the Hell into which he descended.

The souls of God's faithful departed were the first to see
the crucified Son of God come among them:
to end their exile, to open their way to the presence of God,
to wake them from their long sleep, to harrow Hell,
to bring the release of redemption to those
who had lived on earth B.C. – Before Christ.

Absent from the earth, the spirit of Christ is among
the other dead, the long-accumulated legions of the dead,
who have awaited this hour of release.

And so the sun rose on the Sunday –
another dawn but a dawn like no other.
An earthquake.
In one moment, in the twinkling of an eye,
a corpse that was dead and buried is reanimated.

Jesus is transfigured, not in a visionary way as on
Mount Tabor, but as we will all be transformed.
The risen body shows forth the best of our humanity,
suffused with the glory of our immortal souls.

The earth quakes with the power of God,
who not only has the power to create a whole universe,
who not only has the power to create humanity,
body and soul, but who can raise the dead to eternal life.
That one historic moment of the resurrection
was indeed earth-shattering.

Why, we should ask ourselves, why did the angel roll away
the stone? It wasn't to let Jesus out! Jesus had left the tomb already.
He was no longer constrained by physical limits.
Later on, when he appeared to the apostles in the Upper Room,
he came through closed doors. So there was no need to roll
away the stone to allow Jesus to leave.
The angel rolled away the stone not to let Jesus out,
but to allow the women in to see its emptiness.

Jesus had risen from the dead and was no longer entombed;
he was out there in the garden waiting till the women came,
waiting for Mary Magdalen. She had been the first to come.
He had seen her in the thin light of dawn but had remained
out of sight.

He saw her run off to fetch the others. He saw them racing
to check her story. He saw them filled with awe and great joy
as they left the tomb, and then he stepped out of the shadows
and came to meet them.

"Greetings", he said and they fell before him, clasping his feet.
"Do not be afraid", he said. "Go and tell my brothers
that they must leave for Galilee; they will see me there."
And so they did.

The disciples of the dead Jesus disappeared, in fear and despair,
faith destroyed. The disciples of the risen Jesus saw him
again and again and took new heart: faith not just restored
but transfigured.

And that was the faith they began to preach –
a faith in life after death, the faith that was preached
ever since by Peter and John and all the rest:
the Easter faith of the Son of God who offered his life
as a sacrifice on the Cross and rose to eternal life.

This is the night when Jesus Christ broke the chains of death
and rose triumphant from the grave.

Chapter 22

They brought to him all who were sick.

The world is full of incomplete and broken people
and it is the first priority of genuine love to deal
with that reality: by restoring those who are ailing,
and by enabling the incomplete to attain fulfilment.

The life of Jesus is a continuous example of efforts
to proclaim those two priorities. He wanted us to grow to
completeness – wholeness, fulfilledness – and he wanted us
to repair the damage inflicted by sin and death. He told us
that God is Love, and that we can only genuinely worship
God if we understand what Love must do.

Love has to be expressed, not in wonderful words,
but in healing deeds. Love must do everything in its power
to enable people to be fulfilled, and it must do everything
in its power to counter misfortune and ill-health.

And the wonderful consequence of such efforts to love
in a practical way is that those who love selflessly actually
complete themselves in the process.

That's why Christianity – genuine Christianity, not
the lip-service sort – has so often been a nursing faith, a faith
that expresses itself best in relieving poverty and healing the sick.
It is more Christian to visit the sick unobtrusively
than to go to church conspicuously.

Genuine faith, genuine prayer, genuine love will always
find their practical expression in caring for those
who need our time and our love.

It is no coincidence that the World Day of Prayer for the
Sick is on the feast of Our Lady of Lourdes – next Tuesday.
Outsiders who look at the phenomenon of Lourdes

often think that those who go there are going mainly
in search of miracles; but the real miracle of Lourdes
is not the occasional mind-blowing cure but the daily reality
of the impact of generous love on the suffering and the sick.

It's the spirit of prayerful generosity which puts itself at the
service of the weak. It's the brancardiers and the helpers,
the bath-attendants and the wheelchair-pushers who are
Mary's secret weapon, because they do for love what
she beckons them to do. Lourdes is a practical expression –
not of seeking after signs and wonders, but of down-to-earth
love in action.

Twice this week I have found wonderful examples
of such down-to-earth love. The first experience was on
Thursday when I visited an Anglican Benedictine convent
in Edgware, which now has a residential home attached to it.

I happened to arrive when the sisters and several of the residents
were in Chapel, and the beauty of it was that what was
being said exactly corresponded with what was being done.
There was no divergence between theory and practice.
The professed love of God visibly found expression
in love of neighbour. It was beautiful and it was inspiring.
The care of the elderly and the sick is the work of Christ.

The second experience was in a hospital in Oxford when
I was having scans to locate the source of problems in my back.
I had a long wait between scans, during which I finished reading
the autobiography of one of my heroes, Sir Nigel Hawthorne,
the great actor who made 'Sir Humphrey' the epitome of the
Whitehall mandarin, whose portrayal of the madness of George III
worked as well in the cinema as in the theatre, and whose
last great achievement was the most moving, most suffering,
most understandable King Lear I have ever seen.

His autobiography is a book written under the pressure
of the cancer from which he died two Christmases ago.

He realised that he was writing to meet a final deadline. From the epilogue we read:

> Through major surgery, radiotherapy, chemotherapy, jaundice, pneumonia and septicaemia, he wrote on, clinging to the best lifeline that he could have been thrown under the circumstances. He finished the last chapter in hospital the week before Christmas, checked it through when he got home and sent it off on Christmas Eve – two days before he died.

And it's a wonderful read, a fascinating story of a career – he was a very late developer – often very funny and often providing unexpected insights. But it couldn't have been written – and this is one of those unexpected insights – if he had not in his final illness been so well cared for by a partner whom he described as "totally selfless, by which I mean that he cares more for others than he does for himself. The way he has supported me . . . throughout the crisis of my illness is living proof of that."

Living proof. That's the phrase that has leapt out at me this week. It's easy to love the beautiful and the healthy, but real love is proved in other ways and especially when life is coming to its end. The way we care for the sick and dying is the living proof of our belief and our love.

Jesus met that test at every point; can we say the same of ourselves? On the World Day of Prayer for the sick we have to make that prayer more than words; we have to make it practical: there has to be LIVING PROOF of love.

Chapter 23

Why are these doubts rising in your hearts?

It really is very peculiar.

An awful lot of people are happy to believe
they can know what's going to happen tomorrow
by reading a horoscope in the paper.
A lot fewer people believe that they can know what actually
did happen two thousand years ago by reading the Gospels.

People find it easier to believe what will happen
in the future than to believe what did happen in the past.
The same people who say they can't possibly believe
all that stuff about resurrection will happily believe
it's going to be a lousy summer for Taurus.

How do people make such choices about what they believe?
Consider the case of Thomas. He was absent when Jesus
appeared to the others after the resurrection.
He clearly saw himself as a level-headed rationalist.

"Ah, you saw a vision, did you, lads? A dead man, living again.
Pull the other one. I'd need to put my finger into the wounds
in his hands before I could believe anything like that."

There were at least ten eyewitnesses who all told Thomas
that they had seen Jesus. Not good enough. Must see for myself.
And eight days later he did – and then he believed.
But as Jesus commented, "You've seen me yourself and so
now you believe in my resurrection – but happy are those
who haven't seen for themselves and even so believe."

The fact is we simply can't check out every fact for ourselves.
In the end, it's a matter of judgement. I trust one source more than
others, I trust one piece of evidence as more dependable than others.

In the case of Jesus, there was nothing written at the time;
the accounts written later are not always consistent.
But what persuades me that Jesus rose again is not that
Mark said so, or John; but that a consensus of several sources
and a strong living tradition provide a credible story.

It's good enough to be a working hypothesis – and the only
way to be certain is to test it to destruction. And testing it
means to live as if it were all undeniably true, and see
whether it all hangs together.

And it does. My faith now is not just what history tells me
in those documents from the first century. My faith is also
what I have thought in my prayers, what I have learned from
the spiritual writers. It's the intuition that comes from
a deeper awareness of human nature; it's the responses of mind
and heart to Shakespeare's *Tempest* and Michelangelo's *Pietà*
and Poulenc's *Gloria*. It's the experience of life going on
beyond death at each bereavement, at each parting of friends.

What I'm saying is that written evidence is not the sole
indicator of faith, that words do not convey everything about faith,
that other people being eyewitnesses is no guarantee of faith.
You need to live a life of faith in order to test it,
and to allow the Holy Spirit access to your heart.

The words of a creed are not faith. Words have to be tested
by life. Words have to be scrutinised by love. Words have
to survive death. And human words need the Word of God.

Jesus persuaded the disciples that he wasn't a ghost
by allowing them to touch him and watch him eat.
That was their privilege. But he continues to persuade me that
he wasn't a ghost by the accumulated experience of a lifetime.
I have lived life believing that he rose from the dead –
and tested that belief in many ways.

Remember the clever schoolboy who was asked what faith was.

"Oh", he said, airily: "Faith is believing what you know perfectly well isn't true." That's not faith. That's stupidity.

When non-believers talk about 'religious faith' they have the same prejudice as that schoolboy. They think faith is irrational, a rather mindless comfort, a running away from reality, a rather disgraceful and defiant declaration of something we don't really believe in our heart of hearts. And what I'm saying is that faith begins in hope, but has to grow beyond that, and can only deepen and develop if every challenge to it is honestly met.

We should never be afraid to argue – the faith can stand all scrutiny. We should never be afraid to acknowledge difficulties. Our strategy was formulated by Jesus himself. He stayed with us. He did not disappear. He took steps to remain present to us.

If we centre our lives on his presence we can't go far wrong. He assured us that we could always recognise him in the breaking of the bread. Every Mass I have been to, every Mass I have said adds confidence to faith.

So, faith isn't some weird wishful thinking. Faith begins at Easter in puzzlement at the empty tomb, and wonderment at seeing the risen Lord.

Faith then becomes the quiet determination to act on what we hope may be true before we know that it is. And that knowledge that it is true comes through living life in God's presence so that everything we do is a means of grace.

All our experiences, in every aspect of life, are grist to the mill, potential sources of grace. And if we live in the way that hope and faith indicate, then our grace will bring us certainty, certainty of heart as well as certainty of mind.

Touch me, and see for yourselves.
Look at my hands and my feet. It is I indeed.

The Requiem Mass for Cardinal Basil Hume took place in Westminster Cathedral on 25 June 1999 and was broadcast live on Radio 3.

Portrait by Jeff Stultiens, 1987, courtesy of the National Portrait Gallery, London.

Chapter 24

Anyone who welcomes you, welcomes me.

On Friday morning I enjoyed one of the greatest privileges of my life, being able to follow both the vocations God gave me.

It's nearly fifteen years since my two decades as a Radio 3 voice ended, and eleven since I was ordained. On Friday my two vocations flowed together and I was providing the radio commentary for the Cardinal's Requiem.

It was a tremendous occasion, the splendour and the colour and the beauty providing a wonderful setting for the humility and simplicity at the heart of it. The Cardinal had famously asked for no fuss for his dying and we'd respected and obeyed that; but his burial was an opportunity for Catholics and many others to reflect on his life and the message he had preached by his example. From my commentary point high up in the gallery I had a birds-eye view of it all – and that was a small compensation for not being able to be one of the concelebrants down below.

I was conscious of how welcome so many different people were being made to feel in that house of God. Most were Catholics of course, but there were many non-Catholics too, both great and small. Lord Runcie and Archbishop Carey led the Church of England contingent, and I was touched to see a man in the uniform of the Salvation Army go up at Communion time to receive a blessing from Cardinal Cahal Daly of Armagh.

And there was one particular moment at Communion which I'll always remember. The concelebrating Cardinals came down from the sanctuary with the ciboria to give the Lord to the faithful. In the very front row of the congregation were

Tony Blair and Bertie Ahern. They stood up together and the Prime Minister moved out into the aisle and then stepped back a pace and beckoned the Taoiseach to go ahead of him to receive. They were both approaching Cardinal Glemp, the Primate of Poland. The Taoiseach held out his hands and received Communion in the usual way and then as he turned away the Prime Minister stood before the Cardinal with his hands crossed across his chest, to receive a blessing. The Polish Cardinal blessed him and reached out and briefly touched his hand in token of greeting. And then the two leaders knelt side by side making their thanksgiving. The courtesy, the understanding was clear for all to see.

And the thought occurred to me that if all men who do not share the same beliefs could behave with such sensitivity and considerateness, how much better the atmosphere in Ireland could be.

Sometimes you hear people argue that it's better to ignore differences and pretend they don't matter. Call Communion 'the bread of brotherhood' and then it wouldn't matter if Mr Blair shared it too. That's a very shallow solution.

If something is of such profound significance to someone as the Real Presence is to Catholics it does not help to belittle that belief by pretending it doesn't really matter.

It matters a great deal. It is at the heart of our faith. If we just wanted to break the bread of brotherhood we could do so in many places and on many occasions – from football matches to pop concerts. And such areas of common enthusiasm are good. But if we believe that the Mass brings us into the sacramental presence of Christ, then receiving Communion is a profound act of faith and can only be done at the altar.

And Mr Blair was recognising the depth of our creed. He was in effect saying: I'm not actually a Catholic myself

but my respect for the belief of Catholics is such
that I will respect this moment for what it is
and I am content to ask for a blessing.

It has of course nothing whatever to do with people's worthiness –
if we had to be worthy to receive we would never receive.
That is precisely why we declare, in the moments before
receiving, that we are not worthy. *Domine non sum dignus.*
Indeed in one sense no Catholic is ever worthy to receive.
Yes, there are those in irregular marriages or relationships,
but there are also all those who are consumed with anger,
or jealousy or bitterness. Unworthiness comes in many guises.

On the other hand, if worthiness were the criterion, then
Mr Blair's family life might be seen as a good example
of a mixed marriage working well. His Catholic wife and elder son
were also in the Cathedral and came up to receive Communion later.
If it were worthy in that sense, few could be deemed more worthy.
But receiving Jesus in Holy Communion isn't something we do
because we believe we're worthy of him.

We do it because we believe He is truly present. We do it as
an act of faith in the full gospel taught by the Catholic Church.
We are manifesting our being in communion with the mystical
body of Christ and with the Vicar of Christ.

We're not just being nourished by the Body of Christ, we are
proclaiming that it *is* the Body of Christ. Catholics receiving
the Bread of Life believe that it is the Real Presence of Christ
and so it is essential to *believe* that, if they are to receive it.

That is why Tony Blair's demeanour and actions
were so appropriate and I'm sure would have gladdened
Cardinal Hume's heart. The Cardinals of Glasgow and Armagh,
of Warsaw and Utrecht and Dar-es-Salaam,
and the Pope's special envoy,
were able to welcome those approaching them in different ways.

They gave Holy Communion to Catholic believers
and they gave a blessing to those showing their respect
for the significance of Catholic beliefs.

It was an object lesson in how to recognise and accept
differences without letting them undermine friendship.
How to be welcoming without pretending that the most
sacred doctrine is not really important.

Chapter 25

Go and find out all about the child

When I joined the BBC in 1965 each radio network
had its own continuity studio in Broadcasting House.
On the announcer's side of the glass I faced a microphone
and had three turntables and a tape deck to hand.
And what I listened to on the speakers on my side
was the output from continuity – what Broadcasting
House was sending to the transmitters.

On the other side of the glass sat my engineering colleague,
the T.O. – technical operator – facing a console controlling
the sources: tape machines, studios, live outside broadcasts.
What he listened to on his speakers was what was actually
being broadcast, coming back to him from the VHF transmitter
at Wrotham. And every now and again – not daily, or weekly, but
regularly enough, I'd see the T.O. suddenly react as if electrocuted.
Transmission was interrupted, and I'd hear him say "Wrotham's off."

What we were sending from Broadcasting House was no
longer reaching the nation. And sooner or later, when the
fault was rectified, I'd have to make one of those po-faced
announcements: "I'm sorry you missed part of *Petticoat Line*,
Grand Hotel, or whatever; this was because of a power failure
at the transmitter."

And last week I heard it happen again. Here we all were,
in church, for the dying moments of 2002, and behind the crib
was my radio, switched on, and carefully tuned to Radio 4 –
but volume down to zero.

All I had to do at 23.59 was to wind up the volume
and we'd all hear Big Ben chiming us out of the old year
and then the first bongs of 2003.

On the dot, I leant down and turned it up – and nothing!
Just the hiss of that radiophonic mush
that means there's no transmission.
"Good heavens," I thought, "Wrotham's off."
It made front page news next day:
"BBC fails to broadcast Big Ben".

Luckily we had our own chiming clock in the church and
in the absence of its grander colleague it ushered in the New Year
well enough. But without Big Ben, I feel it's a bit like Hamlet
without the Prince of Denmark.

And as the Mass continued, I thought what an excellent parable
was in front of me. It was like those two sets of loudspeakers
in Continuity – mine and the technical operator's –
used for monitoring what was leaving us
and what was coming back from the transmitter.

I am a broadcaster of the Good News – and what's leaving me
is fine – studio output O.K. But to reach the listening audience
it needs transmitters. As it leaves me, it's a narrow-cast, just a line
to Wrotham – what it requires then is a broad-cast from there
and other satellite transmitters.

If the news is to be heard, the announcer is not enough.
It needs transmitters. And that is you – you are the ones
who enable the Good News to be heard.

The world is looking for a purpose: it's looking for fulfilment;
it's looking for Paradise Lost.

And the way we lead our lives is crucial. If I am melancholic,
and mournful, dispirited and gloomy, angry and fed-up,
people say "What's his problem?"

But if I radiate gentleness and peace,
if I radiate honesty and integrity, if I radiate optimism and fulfilment,
if I radiate simple happiness and being fully alive, then, people say
"What makes him tick? What's his secret? What's his faith?"

The Gospel itself, going out from the Bible, and from that wonderful
Continuity studio we call the Church, is actually wonderful news.
But from Continuity it has to go to the transmitters –
and it's up to you.

What signals are you sending to the world around you?
Are you saying in all seriousness what Herod said in
murderous irony: "Go and find out all about the child."

Anyone who is trying to tune in to the goodness of God,
to the beauty of creation, to the harmony of the whole man,
to the perspective of forgiveness;
anyone trying to tune in to all of that
can only get the right signal
if the transmitter is functioning properly.

Over to you.

Chapter 26

I will preserve the offspring of your body after you.

I never had any problems with the first question in the old Penny Catechism. Who made you? God made me.

It seemed to me as a child perfectly straightforward and I've never doubted it as an adult. But the second question was a bit more complicated. I should explain that, from pre-nursery days, I was always known by one of our old family friends as 'Little Why'. Because whenever he told me something, my response was invariably "Why?"

As a very little boy, it seemed to me that 'Why' was my best reaction to the statements and directives of the grown-up world. It seemed to me then the necessary question, and still does today. I'm always telling my confirmation candidates that it is the word they must keep using: *Why?*

If we are to enjoy new insights into our faith, we must positively seek understanding by asking again and again: Why? Why is that so? Why should that be? *Fides quaerens intellectum.*

The present Holy Father marked the twentieth anniversary of his accession with an encyclical on Faith and Reason in which he praises St Anselm of Canterbury for underscoring the importance of asking why. The intellect has to seek what it loves. The more it loves, the more it desires to know.

My childish instinct to ask *why* was supported by the second question in the Penny Catechism. *Why* did God make you? It was a good question – but I wasn't altogether happy with the answer provided.

Why did God make you?

God made me to know Him, love Him and serve Him in this world and to be happy with Him forever in the next.

Now, as a child, I was delighted with the second half of the answer – being happy with him forever. The prospect of the beatific vision meant that dying is no more than a change of life. Death is not the great terminus. There is an ultimately rewarding future to set alongside the other purpose of fulfilment on earth through knowing, loving and serving the Creator.

But it did not occur to me then that the first half of the answer was a bit ambitious. To know God is a very big adventure. At first the optimism of childhood came to my aid. I could see every prospect that my attempts to be friendly with God would produce an equally friendly response from God and that our initial nodding acquaintance would one day deepen into a genuine knowledge.

But later in life, I wasn't so sanguine. By then I'd realised how difficult it is to know someone, *really* to know someone. And I realised that it seemed literally infinitely more improbable that God could expect me to know him, certainly not in this life.

For many years as an adult I thought that God would always be beyond knowing in this world and that I could only aspire to know Him in the next. It was a chance remark, uttered by an American rabbi in the often hostile play, *Angels in America*, that helped me to see that 'to know' someone isn't just a matter of historical data or biographical research.

"So I do not know her – and yet I know her."

It's more a recognition, a perception, an understanding at an instinctive level that enables me to say of someone I love: "Yes, I know him."

It's true of humans; it's also true of God.
I will always be singularly lacking in detailed awareness
of the depths of God's being but, yes, I do know Him.

Faith seeks understanding, but it is the practice of love which
produces that instinctive knowing which transcends mere facts.
No human being who loves another could possibly enumerate
or express all the details of the Beloved, but he can still *know*
his love. And in that same way, that loving way, yes, I can
know God in this world.

So eventually I was able to accept that answer of the
catechism, though perhaps it might have been better
to put knowing God *after* loving and serving Him because,
it seems to me, it is *through* the loving and serving Him
that the knowing Him comes.

For most of my adult life I took that second catechism answer
on trust. Even though it still seemed to me to fail to answer
the question: Why? Why did God make me?

I could understand that loving him, serving him, even knowing
him was a good thing for me to do once I'd been created.
But it didn't really answer the question – why?
Why did God make me? What was his motive?
What was in it for Him?

By now I was immersing myself in literature and history
and realising that their real fascination lies in the discovery
of motivation. It might be Shakespeare probing the motives
for Leontes' eruption of jealousy, or Eamon Duffy disentangling
the motives of an extraordinary succession of popes.

Literature and history demand to know *why* people do what
they do. And for the life of me, I couldn't really understand
what possible motive God could have for complicating
his life by creating me.

The facts of creation are incidental. It doesn't make much difference whether God created the universe in the fundamentalists' six days or in the fashionable Big Bang. That's a matter of *how* he did it. I still wanted to know *why* he did it. Why create me when all his hopes for me were doomed to mean grief for him? Why create humanity, knowing it would have to be redeemed? Why create a world which owed its being to him but which did not recognise him? Why try to add to the perfect relationship of the Trinity, relationships imperfect and inadequate?

For years I presumed that this was really a *mysterium fidei* that I would have to wait until my own eternity before I could understand. The penny dropped long after I was an adult, long after I was a priest. It dropped while I was talking with engaged couples. How tremendous their love for one another, the way they spoke about one another, the affection, the considerateness, the tolerance, the cherishing, the sheer wonder of love.

I have loved too and could recognise authentic love when I met it. But the conversation necessarily moves on when marriage is the enterprise. It moves on from husband and wife to father and mother. And the mere celibate can only marvel that while they are so clearly personifying the highest form of human love, they are also contemplating a major upheaval. They're proposing to wreck the whole thing, compromise the entire set-up, by creating a third party who will be utterly lacking in considerateness, a third party who will ruin their sleep patterns, jeopardise their finances and risk driving a wedge of divided loyalty between them. It's as well not to be too starry-eyed about starting a family!

Why do they do it? I hear one answer to that when I visit the home before the baptism. The earthquake has happened.

The memory of the labour may be receding but the world is irrecoverably upside down – and what I hear is a sort of pride. The father looks at the little creature in the cot with the sort of look that says "I did that" and jokingly says – "With legs like that he might play for Aston Villa".

Can this, I wonder, be the motivation for creation? If it is true that we are made in the image of God can it be the pride of parenthood which provides the clue to God's motive in creating us? Can it be that in the eternal scheme of things, there is divine pride in creation? I'm sure there is – but when I think about it, I realise that pride is a consequence of creation rather than a credible motive for it.

And then the mother looks at this being she has carried within her, at this person she knows in the way that one can know a complete mystery. And she says: "Isn't she lovely, Father, I think she has her Daddy's eyes."

And there it is; there is the motive. There is the reason why God the Creator went outside the Trinity and created us. Humans have the joy of extending the being of the one you love, so that when you are laid to rest with your ancestors, God will preserve the offspring of your body after you.

The mother looks at her child and sees how it continues and prolongs the existence of all she loves in the father. Not pride. Love. The parents see in their offspring a genuine fruit of their love. It's not pride in cloning oneself. It's love, delighted at the prospect of extending what it loves.

That is the real joy of creation, the deep motive for parenthood. God the Father loved the Son so much that he longed to create others in his likeness.

As the penny dropped, I remembered that wonderful sentence in one of the Sunday prefaces:

"You sent him as one like ourselves, though free
   from sin, that you might see and love in us
   what you see and love in Christ."

There in a nutshell is the answer to my question.
When we call God our 'Father' we are recognising in God
what we can identify through experience of human parenthood.
The joy of creating new life derives from being able
to extend into the new life the love of our heart.
It's only superficially that the baby compromises the love
of father and mother. It's only at first glance that the creation
of humanity compromises the love within the Trinity.
The creation of new life is love's delight in extending
what is seen and loved in the Beloved.

God made me to know him, love him and serve him in this
world because he sees and loves in me what he sees and loves
in Christ. And as Christ, the Loved One, is his son in eternity,
so I am his adopted son, created and destined for eternity.
Thus it is that we identify Jesus as our brother and with him
recognise God as Our Father. He gives us the right to become
children of God, not born of any human stock, or by the fleshly
desire of a human father, but the offspring of God himself.

The idea that God chose to create us as extensions of his love
for his own son is crucial to our faith, and to our life on earth.
We echo the words of James Edmeston:

   Lead us, heavenly Father, lead us
      o'er the world's tempestuous sea;
   guard us, guide us, keep us, feed us,
      for we have no help but thee,
   yet possessing every blessing
      if our God our Father be.

*The restored Gothic church beside Kylemore Abbey in Connemara.
This extraordinary miniature echo of Norwich Cathedral
has been cared for by the Benedictine nuns.*

Chapter 27

The kingdom of heaven is like treasure hidden in a field.

Someone met me in Waitrose this morning and said,
"You do look well. You look as if you've been to the
south of France."

"No," I said, "the west of Ireland!"

I've had two wonderful weeks and they felt like an insight
into eternity, and that − when you think about it − is exactly
what a holiday ought to be. It's a rest, of course, and I needed that.
And it's a great help that, where most places have 24-hour days,
in the west of Ireland they last infinitely longer!
The sun doesn't go down till after dinner.
And that was great.

My holiday was in two parts. The first week was spent based
in Sligo with my sister and her son, and we commuted practically
every day through Roscommon to Leitrim. My nephew was
seeing for the first time places he'd often heard his Gran talk
about and meeting people connected with her through ties
of family and friendship. So it was great for him.

And our principal purpose was to complete my mother's story
by taking her ashes back to the scenes of her greatest happiness.
Not sad at all. We had a sense of completeness.

Earthly life is precious from birth to grave and so all the places
where we've been happy have a particular value. And we know
that whenever we go back to Lough Allen we'll have a particular
awareness of the life that was anchored so happily there.
It's as if we can always hear the echo of her words, and sense
the reasons for her faith and understand the forming of her
personality in the shadow of Slieve an Ireann.

For us it will always be a place of pilgrimage, a holy place.

When you look at the word 'holiday', you see that it really
means 'holy day', and a holy day is a day that restores you
to wholeness. You feel complete. You feel at one with
creation. You feel integrated into God's providence.
You see the meaning of your life and how God has loved you.
That's the purpose of a holy day and a place of pilgrimage.

King Solomon had many advantages, but what he asked of God
was something more enduring. He didn't ask for long life,
or riches, but for a discerning heart.

Note – he didn't ask for a clear *mind* to *debate* between good
and evil – it's not the intellectual choices that really matter:
it's the choices we make in our hearts: what – and who – to love.

And so the Lord gave Solomon a heart wise and shrewd –
and that was the gift my mother had too, and the gift I long
to inherit. To be able to feel that your heart beats in time
with the heart of God.

So that first week of the holiday centred on the lovely lake
in Leitrim where the heart can learn to understand how to be
whole. And the second week was even happier than the first.
My sister and her son returned to England and into the tiny
airport at Sligo flew a friend of mine who'd never travelled
in that part of Ireland before. And there is an immediate joy
in being able to share with someone you love places that have
become part of your own lifescape, places that have become
so precious down the years.

We stayed three days in Westport and went up to the top of
Minaun and right out to the beach of Keem on Achill.
We drove alongside the Black Lake towards Killary Harbour and
Leenane and visited the restored gothic church in Kylemore.

And finally three days in Clifden where I really did feel
I was returning to a place where I'd buried a crock of gold –

a store of memories – and was now able to return and dig up the treasure and share it.

But it wasn't simply nostalgia. I go back to that definition of what a holiday really is: of having the time and space to take stock, and put things in perspective and see the world as God sees it and feel integrated into his purpose. It's that security of being a complete being, a whole person, that is crucial. A holiday in its deepest sense is not just recreation but re-creative. We wandered along the miles of empty beaches in Connemara. We sat in a coffee shop in Roundstone, revelling in the ever-changing cloudscape over the Twelve Bens.

And God's continuing creation created harmony *within*. I thought of the words of the hymn: "Mine is the sunlight; mine is the morning", because of that deep-down awareness of God's recreation of the new day.

The need is to see the world through God's eyes, to see love through God's eyes, to be at one.

I said Mass each day, of course – but not in a church. I said a house Mass, in a hotel room, with my companion and navigator taking on a new role as altar-server. And as you contemplate the Mass against such a beautiful backdrop in such a re-creative context, you understand its meaning afresh.

The wonder of the Incarnation – God in his love sharing our human existence. The sacrifice of Christ – giving up that human life for love of us. The gift of the Eucharist showing his determination to be here with us. Then life falls into place and the heart is renewed and restored.

I got in first with my holy days. Now I wish you all, in your turn happy holy days.

*The springtime of youth – a photograph taken
by Brian Harrison at Blenheim Palace on 13 March 1959:
John Eccles, Geoffrey Holland and Cormac Rigby. John was the friend
who shaped my life at university. He died at Aylesbury on 1 January 1964.*

Chapter 28

He took fright and began to sink.

It's easy enough to realise that Peter's faith wasn't as strong as he thought it was. And it indicates to us a very important truth.

Faith is all or nothing. You either believe or you don't believe. Yes, of course there'll be fears and doubts – it wouldn't be faith without them – but the total commitment of faith is the essential.

Modern man doesn't much go for that. He prefers to talk of the balance of probabilities. He rather likes the word 'agnostic' because it sounds terribly sensible and well-balanced, and doesn't commit himself to anything that might be a bit awkward.

That's a delusion. The opposite of faith is unbelief, and 'agnostic' isn't a moderate half-way house between blind faith and no faith. Agnosticism is unbelief, and it is just as unbelieving as not believing. Faith may well suffer from occasional collywobbles, but the commitment is there: I believe; help thou my unbelief.

And that's where Peter came unstuck. He was impetuous and eager and jumped out of the boat but as soon as his feet touched water he didn't believe, and he sank. It was no good because it wasn't total. Faith has to be a hundred per cent. Anything less, and it's not faith.

We have to remember that at the time of this episode, Peter hadn't got much to build his faith on. Jesus had not yet taken him and James and John up the mountain to reveal himself transfigured. That vision – designed to help him cope with the scandal of the Cross – that vision wasn't really enough even so to prevent Peter from failing in faith again three times before the cock crew.

It was only after the Resurrection, when Peter had seen the Lord's dead body drained of blood and then seen his risen body after Easter, that Peter the man of little faith became Peter the Rock of Faith. And that, I think, is important for us.

It's often asked why so many young people full of ideals and good intentions, decent people, lapse from the practice of their faith as they become young adults. Well, there are many explanations. But one of them is that at that stage they have not had to face up to the meaning of death and the purpose of life.

Religion seems just a matter of social convention, doing decent things for the community – and you can do that perfectly adequately without having to go to Mass every week. But religion isn't doing good. Religion is Faith. And faith has to be complete. You have to believe that life is the prelude to eternity and most young people even though they've heard it and repeated it haven't often met it head on.

In one way, I was very blessed. Because I did have to face the question when I was only just through college – and it changed my life. In November 1963 the friend who had shaped my life at university was badly mangled in a car crash. He died on New Year's Day 1964.

What I understand now is that in those weeks of being beside him in intensive care and in the months of coming to terms with it, my gift of faith was being given to me. I prayed from the bottom of my heart that he'd come through it and I was heartbroken when the prayer seemed to have been ignored.

I was faced with the question of what I actually believed. It was simple really. I looked at his beauty so cruelly marred and prayed it might be restored. And it wasn't. He was dead. Did that mean he no longer existed? That was the testing question. I'd been brought up Catholic; I knew about the resurrection;

did I really believe it? Did John exist only for twenty years? Is he now only an echo, a memory?

Looking at that wonderful life so stupidly wasted, was there any point in love? Knowing that he would never speak to me again – was he extinguished, snuffed out? Did the destruction of his mortal life mean that his entire being was destroyed? Or did he continue to live and would we in another dimension be together again?

And I realised I was certain he still lived. I'm still certain now that he lives. I've never doubted it for a moment. That complete recognition that human beings come through death to a different sort of life – that is real faith.

The morning star which brightened my youth became tragically an evening star beckoning from a different direction. But star it still is. He lives. Because we all live. And in that process of understanding, of seeing death as a change not a terminus, I began the lifelong process of faith seeking more and more understanding.

We're not talking mind–over–matter stuff. It's not whether or not someone can walk on hot cinders or walk on water. That's what Peter thought faith was all about at the time of this incident. What it's really all about is the purpose of life itself and our final destiny.

Without love, creation has no explanation. But if love is the explanation there can't possibly be extinction. Love does not create in order to destroy. We are held in existence by eternal love.

Peter eventually saw the truth of that when he ran to the tomb of Jesus and found it empty, when he saw the Risen Jesus eating fish on the lake shore.

That's what our religion is really all about: what happens to us when we die. We tend not to think about it until death tries to assert itself against us. Which is why for most people in their teens and twenties the question hasn't arisen. Religion is boring because it doesn't seem relevant to living – fast living. It's only later on that its relevance becomes clear when we have to consider the end of living.

Faith becomes relevant when love is torn out of the sky by death. And then what do you believe? It hurts terribly – but that's the separation. Separateness hurts.

But faith knows with absolute certainty that the separation is not permanent. Death is not permanent. And you either believe it or you don't. You can't be agnostic about it. You either think that life is a mockery, a brief candle easily snuffed out, or that life is safe in God's hands.

I believe what the Church teaches. Perfect love created life and keeps life in continuous creation right through the watershed of death. Peter sank because at that time he thought it was all a matter of good living and mind over matter – and because he had not yet seen the Risen Lord.

We do not sink.
We are not overwhelmed, because we have seen Him.

> May we, and all who sleep in Christ,
> find in his presence light, happiness and peace.

Chapter 29

Brothers, we wish you happiness; try to grow perfect;
help one another.

One of the worst weeks in the last five years of my mother's life was while she was in Mount Vernon Hospital. Not really the hospital's fault. She was the victim of a fellow-patient.

There was this elderly lady who wouldn't stop in her bed, but flitted around the ward – tidying up. The nurses had their hands full trying to stop her gathering up people's possessions and popping them in the waste bags. And unfortunately, one day while Mother was nodding off, one of the things she tidied away into a waste bag was Mother's hearing aid.

She'd needed one from her fifties. With it she could manage pretty well. Without it she was lost. And on this occasion, it was the best part of a week before a new one could be fitted. I remember poor old Arthur Sudbury going to visit her and his gentle voice was no use at all, and I found the notes he'd written to her.

Misery for a whole week. And then, thank God, they got her a new one and we were back to normal. It was then only the familiar problem when the battery began to run down.

As soon as I realised she'd just answered a wrong question:
"Did the doctor see you this morning?"
"It was in the local paper last week."
I'd take the hearing aid and put in a new battery
and pop it back: "Is that better?" And she'd say,
"You don't need to shout, I'm not deaf."

Being without hearing is a deprivation that can break your heart, because it makes it so difficult to make contact with others. People see a white stick and are rightly sympathetic. But an ear trumpet or a hearing aid doesn't evoke the same response.

I sometimes try to imagine my life without being able to
hear music, missing out on the dawn chorus, failing to hear
a whispered word of love. And it's a dreadful prospect.
I really do think I'd rather lose my legs than my ears.
I could make do without sight as long as I could still listen.

Mother taught me how valuable our hearing is. And it's
one of the ways we can help one another virtually every day.
Showing patience and understanding towards the deaf
is a real test of love.

As you will know, preaching in this church is sometimes
a real test of concentration against a cacophony of child noise.
But what a wonderful noise child noise is – I don't mean
children being stroppy; I mean the ordinary orchestra of
childish hubbub such as we get at the ten o'clock Mass.
It's lovely, that noise, because it's made in the house of God.

There's one persistent noise that can be very apparent at
the 8.30 Mass on Sundays. We've one little lad who was
born profoundly deaf, unable to hear anything at all –
can you imagine the silent isolation of such a child.

I've prayed alongside his parents that the best medical treatment
would rescue him from that isolation.
And it's beginning to work. He's had operations, implants,
and now he has to learn at four years old what other children
have absorbed gradually all through their babyhood.
And sometimes in the excitement of discovering how much
he can hear himself, he provides me with major competition –
and when I hear him carrying on, making his noise so unquietly,
my heart is singing, because this is an answer to prayer.
Of course, if you're trying to listen to a convoluted sermon
when he starts his vocal exercises, it can be a little disconcerting.

But of one thing I am absolutely certain – that what Ross is trying
to say is far more pleasing to God than what Fr Cormac is trying

to say. Because he is discovering what it is to hear and what it is to make sounds – and that discovery is the answer to our prayers.

It can be heart-breaking for the parents of such a child to make the effort to bring him to Mass, Sunday after Sunday, despite all the problems, and to hear people who haven't a clue about those problems tut-tutting and shushing and glaring at him.

Helping people isn't just offering an arm to a blind man crossing the road, helping people is accepting that a profoundly deaf child hasn't much clue about volume control, and doing everything possible to make the child and his parents feel welcome and at home in the house of God.

Yes, I know that the easiest solution would be for the parents to keep him at home and allow us to worship in our nice tidy way, with no distractions, with no reminders of the realities of life. But that nice tidy solution would be a confession of failure: failure to love, failure to understand, failure to imagine what it's like for a child to be profoundly deaf.

Whenever I hear him revving up, I move a little closer to the microphone so I can give him a good run for his money, and I'll do my best to win. But if he does drown me out now and then, I remember how awful my mother's life was in that short week of accidental isolation, and I revel in Ross's noisiness as an almost miraculous answer to prayer. I can echo what St Paul wrote:

> Ross, we wish you happiness – try to grow perfect;
> help us to understand how we can help you.

"The midmost hangs for love" – the effect of three crosses created by the lighting of the hanging crucifix in Most Sacred Heart, Ruislip.

Chapter 30
The midmost hangs for love

A meditation for Passiontide
Ealing Newman Circle, 10 April 2003

My starting point is one of the poems in A E Housman's cycle, *A Shropshire Lad*. It's called 'The Carpenter's Son'.

> Here the hangman stops his cart:
> Now the best of friends must part.
> Fare you well, for ill fare I:
> Live, lads, and I will die.
>
> Oh, at home had I but stayed
> Prenticed to my father's trade,
> Had I stuck to plane and adze,
> I had not been lost, my lads.
>
> Then I might have built perhaps
> Gallows-trees for other chaps,
> Never dangled on my own,
> Had I but left ill alone.
>
> Now, you see, they hang me high,
> And the people passing by
> Stop to shake their fists and curse;
> So 'tis come from ill to worse.
>
> Here hang I, and right and left
> Two poor fellows hang for theft:
> All the same's the luck we prove,
> Though the midmost hangs for love.

Comrades all, that stand and gaze,
Walk henceforth in other ways;
See my neck and save your own:
Comrades all, leave ill alone.

Make some day a decent end,
Shrewder fellows than your friend.
Fare you well, for ill fare I:
Live, lads, and I will die.

In my previous parish, Most Sacred Heart in Ruislip, there's
a crucifix suspended above the old high altar, and the wall
behind the altar is curved. Spotlights on either side illuminate
the crucifix – and the shadows they cast on the curved back
wall recreate the image of the three crosses on Calvary.
The crosses of two thieves, and in the centre the cross of Christ.
Whenever I see it, that phrase of Housman comes to mind:
"The midmost hangs for love".

Even the pagan eye can see that Jesus of Nazareth was no common
criminal. His crime was to have challenged the earthly powers of
Rome and Jerusalem. Well, that may have been his crime – but what
was his motive? Why was he prepared to hang and suffer there?
He was shedding his blood for a different purpose. He was offering
a sacrifice. Not one of those repugnant sacrifices of animals which
characterise biblical worship but the free offering of his own life.
A self-immolation. A self-sacrifice.

It's clear from reading the prophets that God was increasingly
fed up with the token gestures of sacrifice. The rituals proclaimed
repentance, cleansing, reform. But men continued to harden their
hearts, to worship false gods, to live by the devil's rules. The temple
sacrifices were becoming a sham, a pretence. God wanted more
than that. He wanted real sorrow, real tears and a real change of
heart. And so he set the example himself. He so loved the world
– notwithstanding all its neglect and defiance of himself – that he
gave the perfect example of forgiveness. His own infinite nature

is pure love, and he decided to put that infinity, that purity,
that love into the human dimension. And so, in the fullness of time,
a child was born – the son of a virgin, the son of God.
The purpose of that Incarnation was not only to demonstrate
in human terms what the phrase 'God is love' might mean,
but to set out in one graphic and comprehensible image the
totality of God's love. This would be no sacrifice of burnt
offerings; this time God offered himself. The word of God
is Love, and it is a love that does indeed dare to speak its name.
The name is Emmanuel, God is with us. God is not just in heaven;
God is not just everywhere; God is with us. Now and forever.

Jesus lived among us; Jesus lives among us; Jesus will be with us
to the end of time. And the amazing thing is that the Son of God
does not appear like an angel, dazzling with spiritual perfection.
Instead, he appears as a baby in a manger, a healer of cripples,
a comforter of widows, a teacher of wisdom, and a victim of sin.
But not a passive victim of sin. Jesus meets evil head-on.
He is a challenger, rejecting sin, willing to go the final step
of self-sacrifice, ready to suffer and die in order to defeat evil
and to complete the perfection of love.

It is easy enough to love humanity when it is behaving itself;
we are in essence beautiful and loveable. But from the Cross
on Calvary, Jesus saw the unlovely face of humanity –
the power-lust, the barbarity, the hypocrisy. And he still
loved humanity. He still loved *us*. He still loves *me*.

> Thou, thou, my Jesus, after me
> Didst reach thine arms out dying,
> For my sake sufferedst nails and lance
> Mocked and marrèd countenance,
> Sorrows passing number,
> Sweat and care and cumber,
> Yea and death, and this for me,
> And thou couldst see me sinning.
>
> *(Gerard Manley Hopkins)*

Love is not blind; love sees all; and still love loves.

We've travelled rather a long way. It's quite a step from Housman to Hopkins! Let's go back a little.

Housman's lad is a reluctant hero. When he faces the gallows, he finds himself regretting that he hadn't lived quietly and unobtrusively:

> Had I stuck to plane and adze
> I had not been lost, my lads.

Good-hearted he was, that young fellow.
And as he came to die, he felt it had been a mistake
to tangle with the evil in the world. He would have been
wiser to have "left ill alone". His motives had been good.
But his fate is a matter of luck: he had as much luck –
or as little luck – as the two thieves.

> All the same's the luck we prove,
> Though the midmost hangs for love.

And he concludes that he would have been better advised to leave ill alone, and therefore to survive. His dying words are a warning to his pals: keep your heads down.

> Make some day a decent end,
> Shrewder fellows than your friend.
> Fare you well, for ill fare I:
> Live, lads, and I will die.

That is the quiet despair of a good man overwhelmed by the evil of the world; rueful, heart-broken even. His simple goodness had tackled evil and had been borne down by it. The Carpenter's son becomes, in Housman's bleak perception, the voice of ultimate human failure.

Jesus of Nazareth, the carpenter's son, who was also the Word of God, did not see his death as failure. It is true that he had gone through an agony of fear and failure

in Gethsemane, but on the Cross what seemed like the
ultimate cry of despair, "Father why have you forsaken me?"
resolves into the recognition that Ultimate Love must
make the Ultimate Sacrifice if it is to achieve its totality.

How unlike the Housman last words are the last words of Jesus.
His last words: "It is accomplished".
His death, because he accepted it for the sake of love,
becomes his apotheosis.

Love risked everything.
Love was slain.
Love rose from the dead.
Love changes everything.

Let us pause for a moment to consider the image of that apotheosis.
The significant thing is that it is not the image of a transfigured
Christ, conversing on a hill top with long-dead Moses and Elijah.
The image of Jesus we hold constantly in front of our eyes
is that of the midmost who hangs for love, the crucified Jesus:

> to the Jews an obstacle
> > that they cannot get over,
> to the pagans madness,
> > but to those who have been called,
> a Christ who is the power and wisdom of God.
> > > (*1 Cor* 1:25)

The image of the crucified dead Saviour is the ultimate proof
of the credibility of Jesus. He made the ultimate sacrifice
because he was determined to achieve the forgiveness of sins.

He knew sinners, he understood sinners, he loved sinners –
and seeing them with absolute clarity he died for them.

What we have to understand
is that the image of Christ on the Cross
is both an eternal state of being and an historical event.

It is the image of the eternal love of the Son for the Father,
a love so total that it can only be adequately expressed
in the language of self-sacrifice.

And it is also the image of that moment in time
when the liberation of humanity was achieved,
when God's perfect friendship became visible
and accessible to us.

God and sinner reconciled.

A world fragmented
by the conflict of many selfishnesses
has to be brought together again
by the selfless power of absolute love.

Our human world
is one of chipped and damaged love,
of unravelling relationships,
of unreconciled differences,
of unhappy memories and scarred hearts.

And if we allow ourselves to become bogged down
in unforgiving resentments and anger
we can never be free spirits.

What Calvary does
is to release us from the bonds of our history,
to bind up the wounds of love,
to heal the injured heart
and to allow God's forgiveness
to recreate our lives.

When we look at the Crucifix
we realise that God's love has no limit,
that his forgiveness opens up a new creation.

In the light of the cross
we can see evil not as a power in its own right

but as a parasite on creation,
    powerful only because
        our selfishness gives it power.

Once we have seen that evil is no true growth
    but only a cancer,
it becomes possible for us
    to liberate our love.

What is broken can be mended,
what is damaged can be restored.
Through the broken heart of Jesus on the cross
comes the wholeness of the new creation.

Our relationship with Jesus transfigures
every other relationship in our lives.

I am tempted to vary slightly the amiable words
    spoken by Puck at the end of
        A Midsummer Night's Dream.

Those dying words of Jesus
    "It is accomplished"
being translated, become:

    "Give me your hearts, if we be friends,
        And Jesus will restore amends."

The cross, we see now,
is not the symbol of defeat and death
but a symbol of the Saviour's love.

    "Love to the loveless shown
        that they might lovely be."
            (Samuel Crossman, d.1684)

In the process of dying for our sake,
Christ has become our greatest friend.

"He came from his blest throne,
salvation to bestow;
but men made strange, and none
the longed-for Christ would know,
but O, my friend, my friend indeed,
who at my need his life did spend."

The divine Redeemer is our human friend.

Nowhere is the value of human friendship more powerfully
perceived than in the writings of the soldier-poets of the trenches.
They struggled to put into words the intensity
of human love, the intensity of loss.

As experienced by Raymond Heywood, it was akin
to being on Calvary at the foot of the cross:

Just now he spoke to me – I heard his laughter,
He knew the joy of life like other men,
One moment after
I heard a moan – a muffled cry of pain
And then . . . and then I saw a crimson stain
Upon the moonlit space where I was kneeling;
A madness o'er me crept, my heart grew numb
And dead to every feeling.

Dear God, can I not stay
And share his cross?
Ah, no! I needs must turn away
Dry-eyed and silent, and from day to day
My heart shall mourn its loss.

Beneath the moon, grief pale, I clasp his hand,
And for a quiet while
I bend above him, and his tired smile
Will linger in my heart until the end . . .

O God! 'tis only they who loved a friend
Can understand!

It is perhaps only at the moment when our love has died,
has been killed, that the full value of our love becomes clear to us.
The uniqueness. The hurt and desolation of the ending of it.
Forty years on, I remember a hospital in Aylesbury:

> I clasp his hand
> And for a quiet while
> I bend above him, and his tired smile
> Will linger in my heart until the end.

The beloved John must have felt like that
when they took Jesus down from the cross.

And perhaps in after years,
John walked alone on Patmos
walked in the hills and the woods and groves
and remembered, as Robert Graves remembered:

> Walking through trees to cool my heat and pain,
> I know that David's with me here again.
> All that is simple, happy, strong, he is.
> Caressingly I stroke
> Rough bark of the friendly oak.
> A brook goes bubbling by: the voice is his.
> Turf burns with pleasant smoke;
> I laugh at chaffinch and at primroses.
> All that is simple, happy, strong, he is.
> Over the whole wood in a little while
> Breaks his slow smile.

The significance of that poem is its title: *Not Dead*.

Not dead. There is a dawning realisation that love is so intense,
so strong, that it cannot die, and must come to life again.
Love dies, but beyond it is the certainty of love's survival.
It's only Thomas who needs to put his finger in the prints
of the nails – the others, inarticulate but convinced,
knew already, that what they had seen was life restored.
The disciples knew instinctively that they were not yet

ready for that life beyond death. Heaven is a place for
selfless lovers and who of us can claim to be utterly
selfless? We have to work on that until the day we die.
But what motivates us to work on it is that 'tired smile',
that 'slow smile', that smile on the face of Jesus as
he whispers: "It is accomplished".

We have to return again and again to Calvary.
It is good in our prayers to go round all the mysteries
of the life of Christ – Joyful, Luminous, Sorrowful, Glorious.
And as we have been recently reminded, the contemplation
of those mysteries is essentially Christocentric. The rosary
is a wonderful aid to prayer. We can use it, each of us, as we
think best – but, as the Holy Father himself noted:

> A fine way to expand the symbolism of the beads is
> to let them remind us of our many relationships –
> in other words, to rise above the mechanical counting
> of words and to think of love, to contemplate our many loves.
> In that way, the beads of the continuity of our lives and
> loves give added depth to our prayer.

> Here the first thing to note is the way the beads converge
> upon the Crucifix, which both opens and closes the unfolding
> sequence of prayer. The life and prayer of believers is centred
> upon Christ. Everything begins from him, everything leads to,
> attains to, the Father.

So how do we envisage Christ?

The face of Jesus we have to see for ourselves. We are not
pinned down by any photograph or contemporary drawing.
We need, in our own mind's eye, to see the face that Jesus
chooses to show to us. It will be different for each of us.
But it will be authentic. The smile of Christ for each of us
is unique but instantly recognisable. And it is important
for us to choose to see that image.

God made his Word incarnate, and the human Christ invites
us to use his humanity to comprehend his eternal divinity.
He invites us to envisage him. Each of us should try to see
him as we want and need to see him. The choice is ours.
He came to earth to invite us to *use* that human nature of his.

The Church has always understood that. In the mediaeval
devotion of the Way of the Cross, we have the episode
where a perfectly ordinary woman, full of compassion
for this tortured man, brought a towel to press on his
bloody and sweaty face. It was an act of love rewarded
by the image of his face remaining on her towel.
The story traces back to the second century, and much
later, in the eighth century the portrait was said to have
been brought to Rome. It's a lovely tradition, and eloquent.
How we would love to see the face of Christ!

I treasure a representation of Veronica's veil done in the
Abbey of St Walburg in Eichstädt in Bavaria. It was presented
by the Mother Abbess to the commander of the American troops
who liberated the abbey at the end of the war against Hitler –
and he in turn presented it to me as an ordination gift.
Its real value comes from the goodness of those who made it
and those who treasured it. We do need, each of us, to treasure
our own image of Jesus in our heart. It's what the first Preface
of Lent tells us to do. As we prepare to celebrate the paschal
mystery by renewing our mind and heart, we are given the
means to contemplate the mystery of Christ.

"As we recall the great events that gave us new life in Christ,"
it says, "you bring the image of your Son to perfection within us."

So here, within us, is where the image of Christ needs to be,
my own perception of Jesus: his tired smile, his slow smile,
his dying gentle smile of triumph as it is accomplished.

Here in my heart I hold my memories,
here in my heart I cherish my loves
here in my heart Christ reigns, the sovereign of my life.

Jesus came to earth to make God visible,
so that we might see him,
so that we might see him with that inward eye
which is the bliss of solitude.

We see from a distance
the three crosses on Calvary, and each of us can see
that the midmost hangs for love
and it is for each of us to make our own close-up
to see that face of God-made-man.

    Lord of the universe
    Source of creation
    Angels adore
    And the heavens applaud.

    Lord of the world
    Embodied in Jesus
    Embodied again
    In the host and the wine.

    Babe in my heart
    Lover on Calvary
    Lord of my being
    And light of my life.

The representation of Veronica's veil bearing the imprint
of the face of Jesus was given by the nuns of St Walburg's Abbey,
Eichstätt, to Major Gerald J Steiner and given by him
to the newly-ordained Fr Cormac.

Chapter 31

They were standing in front of the throne
and in front of the Lamb.

Twice this week, on Tuesday and on Friday, I was not
scheduled to say Mass in this church. On Tuesday
I was away and on Friday at an in-service training day.
The Masses here were covered by Fr Peter and Fr Philip
so there was no loss to the parish.

But since 1958 I have been a daily Mass man. A day
without Mass is a day without sunshine, without food,
without purpose. So what do I do when I'm not able to
say a normal public Mass? Often, as several of you know,
I seize the opportunity to say a house Mass in the home
of someone who maybe finds it hard to get to Mass.
But on Tuesday and Friday the timetable precluded that.

So what did I do? I got up half an hour earlier and
said a private Mass with only myself *apparently* present.
On Tuesday, a house Mass; on Friday, here in the church
at seven in the morning.

I say with only myself apparently present. There is a
marvellous story of the Venerable Bede as an old man
in his monastery in Jarrow. He was close to the end
of his long scholarly life, working diligently to finish
one of his New Testament commentaries before he died.
So frail that he couldn't be expected to go down to the
Abbey church for the monastic services. But he said Mass
in his cell while the others were at Mass in the church.

The young novice who'd been assigned to look after him
decided to slip out of the main chapel during the Offertory
just to pop up and check that the old fellow was alright,

and as he hurried along the passage he could see a light
much brighter than the two candles he'd lit for Bede.
He looked through a crack in the door of Bede's cell.
Bede was saying Mass – with a congregation of angels
and saints invisible to the human eye, but filling the cell
with a dazzling radiance by their presence and joining in
the responses to the Mass.

The young monk stole away again, back to the main chapel,
realising that when Mass is being said, the congregation
is much greater than he'd imagined.

I have never forgotten that story of St Bede, and when
I say Mass I'm aware that it's not a private devotion; nor
is it just the coming together of the people of God here
and now; it's the expression in time of the eternal sacrifice
the Son offers to the Father; it reaches from eternity to us
and it concerns not only us who are physically present,
but all who are saved by the blood of the Lamb.

What does that mean in practical terms? It means that
whenever we are at Mass we are opening a dialogue
with eternity; we are identifying ourselves
as part of the communion of saints.

So on Friday morning I was standing at the altar,
apparently alone, about to start the Mass.
As I made the sign of the cross the church filled
with unseen presences, many of them unknown to me.
But I'd made a point of inviting Mother and Paddy Healey
to be there. I could see the places in the church where
they often knelt and I've no doubt they were there.
The Mass drew them here as it drew them here in life.

The priest offering the sacrifice of Christ is never alone.
He's aware of all the saints, all the angels, choosing to be
with him at that Mass. He's aware that during the Mass

he is closest to the world of the spirit, closest to the heart of God, closest to those God loves.

One final thought. There'll be some who find this fanciful, rather a bit of wishful thinking, wanting the dead to be present. Let me tell you this: I look at you during Mass and I can often see that though you are physically present, your mind is elsewhere, you're not really here.

On the other hand I'm aware that during Mass there are others whom I can't see, but who are really here, heart and soul and mind – the saints.

We celebrate the feast of All Saints today; they're not 'up there'; they're alongside, present with God, present with us.